ON THEOLOGY

ON THEOLOGY

Schubert M. Ogden

1817

Harper & Row, Publishers, San Francisco

Cambridge, Hagerstown, New York, Philadelphia, Washington
London, Mexico City, São Paulo, Singapore, Sydney

The author thanks the publishers who have generously granted permission to reprint previously published material: "What Is Theology?" was originally published in *Journal of Religion* 52 (1972): 22–40, and is reprinted with permission; "On Revelation" is from *Our Common History as Christians: Essays in Honor of Albert C. Outler*, edited by John Deschner, Leroy T. Howe, and Klaus Penzel, copyright © 1975 by Oxford University Press, Inc., reprinted by permission; "The Authority of Scripture for Theology" was originally published in *Interpretation* 30 (1976): 242–261, and is reprinted with permission; "The Task of Philosophical Theology" is reprinted from *The Future of Philosophical Theology*, edited by Robert A. Evans, copyright © 1971 The Westminster Press, reprinted and used by permission; "Prolegomena to Practical Theology" was originally published in *Perkins School of Theology Journal* 35, 3 (Summer 1982): 17–21, and is reprinted with permission; "Theology and Religious Studies: Their Difference and the Difference It Makes" was originally published in *Journal of the American Academy of Religion* 46 (1978): 3–17, and is reprinted with permission; "Theology in the University" was originally published in *Unfinished Essays in Honor of Ray L. Hart*, edited by Mark C. Taylor, *JAAR Thematic Studies*, 48/1 (1980): 3–13, reprinted with permission; "The Concept of a Theology of Liberation: Must a Christian Theology Today Be So Conceived?" was originally published in *The Challenge of Liberation Theology: A First World Response*, edited by Brian J. Mahan and L. Dale Richesin (Maryknoll, NY: Orbis Books, 1981): 127–140, reprinted with permission.

FIRST EDITION

Library of Congress Cataloging-in-Publication Data

Ogden, Schubert Miles, 1928–
　On theology.

　Rev. versions of essays originally published 1971–
1982.
　Bibliography: p. 151
　Includes index.
　Contents: What is theology? — On revelation — The authority of scripture for theology — [etc.]
　1. Theology. I. Title.
BT80.039　1986　　　　230　　　　85-51999
ISBN 0-86683-529-6

86　87　88　89　90　HC　10　9　8　7　6　5　4　3　2　1

To
My Colleagues at The Divinity School
Crescat scientia, vita excolatur

Contents

Preface

The conviction underlying the following studies is that the question, What is theology?, is itself a theological, not merely a pretheological, question. Consequently, from their standpoint, pursuit of this question can be allowed to be a matter of so-called prolegomena to theology only insofar as one agrees with Karl Barth that "prolegomena" means not the things that are said *before* one does theology, but rather the things that are said *first*, once one is already doing it. Of course, to believe that this question is already theological is not necessarily to believe that it is only theological, in the sense that an adequate answer to it requires special criteria of truth or special qualifications of theologians. On the contrary, as the studies together seek to show, any such understanding of theology is as unnecessary as it is problematic. Even so, because the question to which they are all addressed is itself theological, they themselves are all properly theological studies in the sense of these words that they jointly serve to explain.

Among the other things this implies is that the burden of the studies, as of theology generally, is both critical and constructive. By this I mean that they together attempt to point beyond all of the usual alternatives for theological self-understanding, revisionary as well as traditional. Since they were originally composed independently, at different times and places and in response to different specific problems, they naturally play somewhat different roles in bearing this common burden. Nor does their having been thoroughly rewritten for inclusion in this volume completely hide the fact that the concepts in which they respectively understand theology are by no means exactly the same. But with all their obvious differences, they each seek to extend the range of alternatives for a constructive understanding of the nature and task of Christian theology. And if their concepts of theology are evidently variable, what is clearly constant in them is the general problematic of achieving just such an understanding in our situation today. Specifically, they are all concerned, in one way or another, to work out an understanding of theology in which it has as much to do with determining the truth of the Christian witness as with determining its meaning and in which theology's service to this witness is nonetheless real for being indirect and nonetheless indirect for being real. Others will have to judge the success of the studies in realizing this project. But I am bold to think that they at least indicate another possibility for reasoned choice; and this, in my opinion, is the critico-constructive function that all theological reflection is supposed to perform.

In reworking these studies, I have become more sensible than ever before of the immense debt I owe to my association with The University of Chicago, where the thought that all learning, including theology, must be allowed to flourish so that life itself may be enriched is more than the motto of the University. For this reason and also because the first study was originally written for a retreat of the faculty of The Divinity School, I have taken the liberty of dedicating the volume to my colleagues there, in gratitude for all the ties that continue to bind us together. And this has seemed all the more appropriate to me because it was one of their number, my friend David Tracy, who first suggested the idea of publishing such a volume.

For the rest, most of the help I have received in completing it will be evident from the works I have cited. But I do want to thank Betty Manning and especially Mary Ann Marshall for processing my manuscript into finished copy.

Rollinsville, Colorado   S.M.O.
August 1985

It is the glory of the Gospel Charter and the Christian Constitution, that its Author and Head is the Spirit of Truth, Essential Reason as well as Absolute and Incomprehensible Will. Like a just Monarch, he refers even his own causes to the Judgment of his high Courts. He has his King's Bench in the Reason, his Court of Equity in the Conscience: *that* the Representative of his majesty and universal justice, *this* the nearest to the King's heart, and the dispenser of his particular decrees. He has likewise his Court of Common Pleas in the Understanding, his Court of Exchequer in the Prudence. The Laws are *his* Laws. And though by Signs and Miracles he has mercifully condescended to interline here and there with his own hand the great Statutebook, which he had dictated to his Amanuensis, Nature; yet has he been graciously pleased to forbid our receiving as the *King's* Mandates aught that is not stamped with the Great Seal of the Conscience, and countersigned by the Reason.

Samuel Taylor Coleridge

1

What Is Theology?

1. *Theology, in the sense explicitly conveyed by the words "Christian theology," is the fully reflective understanding of the Christian witness of faith as decisive for human existence.*

One of the defining characteristics of theology, which it shares with philosophy in contrast to the special sciences, is that it necessarily includes reflection on its own conditions of possibility as a form of understanding. Thus the question of what theology is is itself a theological question whose answer is subject to the same criteria of adequacy as any other theological answer. For reasons that will presently become clear, the theological understanding of theology peculiarly coincides with the philosophical understanding, with the result that it is applicable in principle not only to Christian theology but also to the theological reflection cognate with any other witness of faith or religion. Islamic theology, for example, may be understood, *mutatis mutandis*, as the fully reflective understanding of Islam as similarly decisive for human existence.

But this primary sense of "theology" is not its only sense. It may also mean an integral part of philosophy's central task as metaphysics, in which case its meaning is explicated by the phrase "philosophical theology" (or, less happily, "natural theology"). This secondary sense is important because reflection discloses that philosophical theology is necessarily presupposed or implied by Christian theology—as well as, naturally, by the theology appropriate to every other religious tradition (see below, pp. 69–93).

As for the phrase "fully reflective understanding," it is intended to describe formally the mode or level of understanding that is properly theological. Since all understanding appears to involve some degree of reflection, "reflective understanding" by itself may understandably be considered a pleonasm. Yet since reflectiveness clearly seems to be a matter of degree, addition of the adverb "fully" results in a significant expression, which makes explicit what is also intended by the unqualified phrase: that reflection is, or should be, present to the highest degree in theological understanding. Implied thereby, of course, is that theology ought to exhibit at least some of the formal marks of any "science," including the methodical pursuit of its questions and the formulation of its answers in a precise conceptuality.

The ambiguity of the genitive phrase "the fully reflective understanding of the Christian witness of faith" is systematic and significant. Since Wilhelm Dilthey, it has been recognized that in the human sciences (*Geisteswissenschaften*), to which theology clearly is most closely related, the relation of the inquirer to the object of inquiry cannot be merely that of subject to object. Because the object of any such science is itself a meaningful human activity, and thus is or involves some mode of understanding, the only criteria of identity finally appropriate for specifying its regularities are those that it itself provides. Consequently, there can be no adequate understanding of such an activity as an object that is not also indirectly its fuller understanding of itself as a subject. It may be argued that the same is true *a fortiori* in the case of theology, since, rather like philosophy, its object is not this human activity or that, but the all-inclusive activity of witness, and thus human existence as such. In other words, the Christian witness of faith can become the object of theological understanding only insofar as it indirectly becomes the subject of such understanding as well. To this extent, there is a sound basis for the traditional formula in which theology is succinctly defined as *fides quaerens intellectum*.

It should also be noted that "the Christian witness of faith" is constituted explicitly as such by the christological claim concerning the decisive significance of Jesus. Consequently, as theology is defined here, it is precisely this claim that is the central object of theological reflection, even as foremost among its data are the various formulations in which this claim has been expressed or implied.

2. *As such, theology presupposes as a condition of its possibility the correlation of the Christian witness of faith and human existence, both poles of which alike have a variable as well as a constant aspect.*

Like all reflective understanding, theology necessarily presupposes its object, which in its case is the specifically Christian witness of faith. But as has been indicated, this witness exists only in correlation with human existence, for which it claims to be decisive. In this, to be sure, the Christian witness of faith is no different from any other, since it is the essence of a religion to advance this claim and, as a consequence, to involve this correlation. As Alfred North Whitehead puts it, "religion claims that its concepts, though derived primarily from special experiences, are yet of universal validity, to be applied by faith to the ordering of all experience. . . . It arises from that which is special, but it extends to what is general" (1926: 32). So, too, with the Christian religion or witness of faith that theology presupposes: it is one expression of existence among others, which nevertheless claims to be decisive for the whole of such existence.

This explains, by the way, why theology can hardly be adequately defined in Martin Heidegger's sense as "a positive science." According to Heidegger, "theology is a positive science, and hence as such absolutely different from philosophy. . . . In principle [it] stands closer to chemistry and mathematics than to philosophy" (15). What Heidegger overlooks is—in Whitehead's words—"the peculiar position of religion," including the Christian religion, that "it stands *between* abstract metaphysics and the particular principles applying to only some among the experiences of life" (1926: 31; italics added). Heidegger himself insists, rightly, that "the scientific character of theology" can by no means be adequately determined simply by taking that of some other science as its standard (26). But the question is whether he does not violate this very rule by tacitly assuming that theology must somehow conform to his general distinction between "positive science" and "philosophy" (= "ontology"). To be sure, he so conceives the defining characteristics of a positive science that they allow for considerable differences among the various sciences that may be thus characterized (16–17). Yet it seems clear that they hardly allow for a positive science having the same completely general scope and absolutely basic status as ontology, even though this is the only kind of positive science that theology could possibly be.

To speak simply of witness and existence, however, evidently involves a high level of abstraction. Neither the Christian witness of faith nor the human existence with which it is correlated is ever given concretely in the way that the terms suggest. The witness is present only in the form of all the various witnesses and kinds of witness, and the same is true of existence—insofar as it can be fully understood only through the whole of human history and all the forms of culture. In this sense, witness and existence alike have variable as well as constant aspects. Consequently, even if the object of theological reflection is one— namely, the one reality of human existence as decisively qualified by the Christian witness—its data are many, and that irreducibly.

3. *Because theological understanding itself must therefore be correlative in structure, it is subject to assessment by dual criteria of adequacy, which are likewise variable as well as constant in their specific requirements; accordingly, to be assessed as adequate, a theological statement must meet the two criteria of appropriateness and credibility as these may require in the given situation.*

If theology is to reflect the correlation involved in the claim of the Christian witness to be decisive for human existence, it itself must be correspondingly correlative in its very constitution. Both as a whole and in each of its parts, it must so interpret its many data as to validate this essential claim. This it can do only by exhibiting the witness of faith as expressive of *the* answer to the one fundamental question expressed or implied by all of human life and history. But this implies in turn that the criteria of theological understanding or, more correctly, of the adequacy of theological statements, are necessarily double.

One such criterion requires that no theological statement be deemed adequate unless it is *appropriate*, in the sense that it represents the same understanding of faith as is expressed in the "datum discourse" of normative Christian witness. A somewhat more technical way of formulating this requirement can be derived from a point made previously. In all understanding of understanding, such as is the task of theology along with philosophy and the human sciences, the only appropriate criteria of identity and regularity are those provided in the first instance by the primary understanding. Although this does not mean that reflective understanding may employ no concepts or assertions other than those of its datum discourse, it does imply that the development of its conceptuality should never lose touch with the symbolism it is supposed to interpret. For this reason, a theological statement may be said to be appropriate only insofar as the understanding expressed by its concepts is that also expressed by the primary symbols of normative witness.

As for the other criterion, it requires that no theological statement be assessed as adequate which is not also *credible*, in that it meets the relevant conditions of truth universally established with human existence. Since this is the criterion whose necessity in theology is likely to be denied or obscured, it is important to remove any doubt as to its derivation.

As we have seen, it is of the essence of the Christian witness that it claims to be decisive for human existence. Implied by this claim, however, is the further claim to truth—specifically, to the truth of the understanding of faith of which the symbols of the Christian witness are the primary expression. Furthermore, this understanding is held to be true because it meets the conditions of truth that are everywhere given with existence itself—as is evident from the fact that the witness of faith appeals simply to "every man's conscience in the sight of God" (2 Cor. 4:2). But this means that the requirement that theological statements be credible, and thus universally true, is far from merely the demand of an alien "rationalism." This requirement is, in fact, the direct reflection at the level of full understanding of what the witness of faith itself essentially demands.

So to state the criteria of adequacy, however, abstracts altogether from the difficulty of applying them. We already touched on this difficulty when we recognized that the data of theological understanding with respect to both poles alike are irreducibly many. Since the one witness of faith is present only in all the many witnesses and kinds of witness, it cannot be easy to determine which statements appropriately interpret it. And so, also, in the matter of what statements are credible; given the vast variety of history and culture, this is even harder to decide. The nub of the difficulty, of course, is that even the criteria themselves are open to variation in their specific requirements. Prior to the development of modern historical consciousness, it could be assumed that agreement with the received understanding of an allegedly infallible scripture or dogma was a sufficient test of the appropriateness of a theological statement. But we now realize only too well that scripture and dogma themselves, as well as any supposed understanding of them, are so thoroughly historical as to render any such test insufficient. Likewise and for the same reason, we now recognize that what one epoch or culture accepts as criteria of truth by no means needs to be accepted by another. As a matter of fact, aware as we are that "uniqueness demonstrations" are hard to come by even in logic and mathematics, we know that even the most fundamental conditions of credibility may be subject to change.

All of this is to say that the two criteria of theological adequacy are situation-dependent as well as situation-invariant in what they require. Although in one aspect their requirements are always the same, in another they are constantly different, contingent on the possibilities and limitations of different historical situations. In general, their requirements in a situation are most likely to be discerned through intensive discussion with its best secular knowledge—in the case of appropriateness, the knowledge of history; in the case of credibility, that of philosophy and the special sciences as well as the various arts. And yet in neither case is a theologian dependent on some other inquirer to specify these requirements. Although, given the situation, the theologian is subject to the same requirements as any other inquirer engaged in logically the same kind of inquiry, he or she has a role to play in determining the requirements; and this role leaves ample room for offensive as well as defensive moves in the discussion with secular colleagues.

4. *Insofar as a theological statement is adequate, and thus both appropriate and credible, it is at once dogmatic and apologetic as well as critical and constructive.*

In other words, such familiar phrases as "dogmatic theology," "apologetic theology," "critical theology," and "constructive theology" are all pleonasms, which are significant only to the extent that "theology" is always open to misunderstanding in one respect or another. Properly speaking, a theology that was not dog-matic would be no theology at all in the relevant sense of the word; for as we have seen, the first requirement of the theology of any religion is that its statements give appropriate expression to the same understanding of faith as is expressed in the nor-mative witness or "dogma" it presupposes as its object. The same would be true of a theology that was not apologetic or not critical and constructive; since it would then fail to be credible or would be in some respect deficiently reflective, it would be lacking in one or the other of theology's essential qualifications and to that extent not really be theology. None of this is to deny, naturally, that in different situations theology may be quite cor-rectly viewed more under one aspect than another—as when, as at present, there is a new appreciation for its inescapable apol-ogetic task, or when the detailed criticism of particular questions is held to be more important than the development of compre-hensive systems.

5. *Although theology is a single movement of reflection, it has three distinct moments which allow for its differentiation into the interrelated disciplines of historical, systematic, and practical theology.*

Up to this point, theology has been considered simply as such and without differentiation to make clear that, behind the complexity of the field as it has developed historically, there is, after all, but one movement of reflection having one integral task. Among other reasons that could be given for emphasizing this is that its recognition is essential for effectively controlling the growth of specialization, which has not always contributed to the advancement of theological understanding.

Still, the unity of such understanding is itself complex, so that the self-differentiation of theology is to a considerable extent natural and of good effect. With all its limitations, the advan-tages of a division of labor are clear, and theology has as much reason to claim them as does any other form of reflective un-derstanding. In fact, it has even more reason, since, from the standpoint of its logic, it is a field-encompassing field. Its unity is a unity-in-diversity involving three distinct moments, each centering in a logically different kind of question. Accordingly, its differentiation into the three main disciplines of historical, systematic, and practical theology is fully allowed for by its own essential constitution.

Yet for all their differences, the three disciplines are thoroughly interrelated in that their respective questions and answers all fall within the horizon of a single inquiry. As Heidegger puts it, "Theology is systematic only if it is historical-practical. Theology is historical only if it is systematic-practical. Theology is practical only if it is systematic-historical" (25). Thus, as we shall see, each discipline is in its own way correlative in structure, and its statements are subject to assessment by generally the same two criteria of adequacy.

6. *Historical theology, which includes exegetical theology as a special case, answers the general question, "What has the Christian witness of faith already been as decisive for human existence?"; as such, it is cognate with all other historical inquiries and subject to common criteria of credibility.*

It is important here to recall the point made earlier that the witness of faith is present concretely only in the form of the many actual witnesses and kinds of witness. By "witnesses" is meant simply the meanings expressed or implied by all the individuals and groups that have in fact borne testimony to the Christian understanding of faith. But *"kinds of witness"* takes account also of the fact that there always have been, because there always must be, any number of ways in which such testimony could be borne. Indeed, it belongs to the very nature of faith that there is no human activity, and hence no form of culture, that does not in some way bear witness to it. In general, however, one may distinguish between the *explicit* witness of faith, which is borne by religion as one form of culture among others, and the *implicit* witness of faith, which is borne somehow by all the remaining cultural forms. To say, then, that the question of historical theology is what the Christian witness of faith has already been is to say that it is concerned with the reflective understanding of the history of the Christian religion, its beliefs, rites, social organizations, and theology, together with the rest of human activity and culture so far as they have been shaped by this witness.

Saying this, however, should already make clear why historical theology is cognate with historical inquiry in general and assessable by the same criteria of truth. The Christian religion is obviously continuous with the history of religion generally, which is, in turn, of a piece with all the rest of the human story. Consequently, to understand Christian history, as historical theology is called to do, is to be engaged in discussion at every point with the general secular study of the religious and cultural past.

Among the other things this implies is that the inquiry of historical theology, also, finally takes place within a larger horizon. Just as study of the past in general is ultimately for the sake of authentic existence in the present and the future, so study of the past as specifically Christian serves the same ulterior end. This is not to deny, naturally, that all historical inquiry, including that of historical theology, has its own autonomous structure firmly grounded in the logically different kind of question it attempts to answer. As a matter of fact, the rule applies here with particular force that the larger cause is best served by those who are free to serve it in their proper way. Still, like all historical inquiries, historical theology is but part of a whole that should to some extent determine its character. In its choice of topics for research it should not only be sensitive to the needs of the entire field, but it should never be content with merely exhibiting the past for its own sake. From this it follows that its most essential task is the provision of accurate and readable translations of significant texts, together with critical interpretations that risk expressing the meaning of these texts in contemporary terms.

All that has been said about historical theology in general fully applies to the special case of exegetical theology. Even the study of scripture is nothing other than historical study, continuous at every point from data to methods both with the study of other Christian tradition and thence with the comprehensive understanding of the entire human past. And yet in the nature of the case, the texts of the Old and the New Testaments have a peculiar place in theological reflection. Like other historical traditions, the Christian tradition is heterogeneous in composition to the extent that, through special acts of self-definition, certain of its elements have acquired a normative significance in relation to some or all of the rest. Unique among such elements is the canon of scripture, which from an early time was judged to be prophetic and apostolic witness to Jesus Christ and which, therefore, in one way or another, has exercised the authority of a universal norm within the tradition—as appears from its historic designation as *norma normans, sed non normata*. Consequently, by far the largest part of the Christian past may be plausibly regarded as the history of scriptural interpretation—provided, of course, interpretation is taken broadly enough to cover not only *theoria* but *praxis*, as well as the rest of human self-expression. Furthermore, the critical interpretation of scripture, toward which the whole of historical theology converges, is just the point of first importance for the other theological disciplines; for with all the difficulties of applying it, agreement with the witness of the apostles that is contained in the New Testament is still the primary test of the appropriateness of theological statements, practical as well as systematic. There can be no question, then, that historical study of scripture is in a way special and that it is sufficiently special to have some claim to constitute a fourth discipline of theological inquiry. If such a claim has not been honored here, it is because the unity of scripture with tradition, and hence of exegesis with historical theology generally, seems an even more important consideration.

Finally, it is by no means accidental that historical theology is the first of the three disciplines to be considered. As Adolf von Harnack rightly insisted, if history never has the last word in theology, it always has the first (Harnack).

7. Systematic theology, including what is sometimes distinguished as moral theology, answers all questions of the type, "What is the Christian witness of faith as decisive for human existence?"; since it therefore consists in a reflective understanding of ultimate reality, it is more or less closely related to all the other systematic inquiries of philosophy and the special sciences and is credible by the same criteria.

Although historical theology itself properly engages in critical interpretation (*Sachkritik*), including the expression of historical meanings in contemporary terms, it still is something different from systematic theology. Nor is the difference simply that historical theology interprets the *many* witnesses and kinds of witness, while it is reserved to systematic theology to essay interpretations of the *one* witness of faith itself. Historical theology has every reason to concern itself with the one as well as the many, and to do so without in the least encroaching on systematic theology. For the real difference between the two disciplines is logical: the difference between expressing what has already been said or meant by others and expressing what is properly said or meant by all, whether or not anyone up to now has ever actually said it. In other words, the distinctive task of systematic theology is to express at the level of full reflectiveness the understanding of faith, and hence the understanding of ultimate reality, decisively attested by the Christian witness.

That the understanding of faith (*genitivus subjectivus*) is also and as such an understanding of ultimate reality (*genitivus objectivus*) hardly requires explanation. "To have faith" is, at the least, "to believe" and thus to be committed to some understanding of the way things ultimately are. Moreover, because the Christian witness of faith claims to be decisive for human existence, it also claims, in effect, to represent the understanding of ultimate reality that is true; this means, as we have seen, the same understanding universally given with existence as such, and thus also properly expressed by the systematic forms of reflection generally. Accordingly, if the claim of the Christian witness is warranted, its systematic interpretation, insofar as it is appropriate to its apostolic norm, should also be credible—in that it both confirms and is confirmed by the cognate understanding of ultimate reality represented by philosophy and the special sciences. In this sense, the achievement of a systematic theology that is credible as well as appropriate is a validation of the claim of the Christian witness to re-present the truth of human existence.

For reasons already given, the possibility of such an achievement is in the nature of the case situation-dependent, in that it is always a matter of the opportunities and limitations of a particular historical context. Yet, clearly, there are also definite limits imposed by the essential meaning of the Christian witness itself. Just where these limits lie is no doubt far more difficult to determine than has commonly been assumed. All sorts of beliefs once held to be essential to the Christian witness have since proved to be inessential, and critically interpreting them has only freed theology for more appropriate interpretations of what faith understands. Still, the Christian witness historically has represented a definite understanding of the nature of ultimate reality—of God, the world, and ourselves—with which certain other understandings are obviously incompatible. This is particularly evident to us today, when the conflict of Christian beliefs with the secularistic claims made by many in our secular culture is undeniable. But even in our situation, the task of systematic theology remains in principle the same: to achieve an understanding of the Christian witness that, however different it may be from all previous witnesses and their theological interpretations, appropriately grasps their essential meaning; and that, with whatever differences from current philosophical and scientific opinions, is credible by the same criteria of truth to which they, too, are subject.

To understand the character of our present situation, however, is to recognize the centrality of systematic theology among the three disciplines. I referred earlier to the peculiarity of theological reflection, which it shares with philosophical, that it is required to reflect on its own conditions of possibility as a form of understanding. Since it is this very possibility that the claims of modern secularism have now made problematic, it is not surprising that theologians have recently had to give considerable attention to the various aspects of this basic problem. Yet, significantly, such reflection has not only commonly been done by systematicians, but is also generally allowed to be the responsibility of their discipline. And this with good reason; for the task of self-reflection, which is essential to theology and which the present situation has made crucial, is quite properly a systematic task. Unlike the special sciences, theology is such that its content and its method are finally not two questions but one. Therefore, it is only fitting that the discipline to which it belongs to express faith's understanding of ultimate reality in concepts that are at once appropriate and credible should also be responsible for the methodology of the entire field. Nor is this the only reason systematic theology occupies a central place. Not only does it reflectively establish the methods of the other disciplines, but it even contributes to their respective contents—in the case of historical theology, by providing the conceptuality required by its critical interpretations; and in the case of practical theology, by providing the first principles necessary to its particular conclusions.

Once again, then, we may note a direct correspondence between the relations of the three disciplines among themselves and their place in our consideration here. In fact, we may well appropriate the suggestion of Heinrich Ott and picture systematic theology as the keystone in the one "hermeneutical arch" of theological understanding (Ott).

8. *Practical theology, which should be understood much more comprehensively than is commonly the case, answers the general question, "What should the Christian witness of faith now become as decisive for human existence?"; accordingly, it is continuous with all other inquiries of the same logical type, especially the human sciences and the various arts, sharing identical criteria of truth.*

Many, if not all, of the handicaps under which practical theology usually labors are due to its being conceived far too narrowly. Ordinarily, the only task assigned to it is to reflect on the shape to be given to the explicit witness of faith through the forms of religion, and this solely in relation to the official functions of the ordained ministry. Significantly, even Heidegger fails to overcome this narrowness in the ordinary conception. Although he argues, correctly, that since "existing" is "acting," and thus "πρᾶξις," "theology by its very nature has the character of a practical science," he takes this to imply simply that theology properly organizes itself as "homiletics and catechetics" (24–25). Thus not only is practical theology generally thought to be of value principally to clergy—present and prospective—but experience in the ministerial office is often supposed to be the main qualification for engaging in it. Not surprisingly, practical theologians frequently strike their colleagues as suffering from real inferiority as well as feelings thereof—their discipline apparently consisting in little more than an assortment of clerical techniques.

But none of this is as unavoidable as its prevalence may tempt one to think. As we have seen, there is vastly more to the witness of faith than the explicit witness of religion, and it is easy to show that the only primary form of Christian ministry is that of the whole people of God. Consequently, there are the best of reasons for striking at the root of practical theology's difficulties by conceiving it much more inclusively—namely, as reflective understanding of the responsibilities of Christian witness as such in the present situation.

Needless to say, such a conception allows for practical theology's still having the task ordinarily assigned to it. Insofar as expression of faith through proper religious forms is an abiding responsibility of Christian witness, practical theology has every right to concern itself with the present possibilities of such expression. Nor is there any reason why it should not give special attention to the functions of the ministerial office, so long as this office remains central to the explicit witness of the Christian community. But on a comprehensive conception of its responsibility, all of this remains but a part—in fact, the smaller part—of practical theology. Its far larger task is also to reflect on the present possibilities of the *implicit* witness of faith in all its different modes. Thus among the most important issues that practical theology today is called to consider are those raised by the role of the community of witness, both gathered and dispersed, in a period of rapid social change and rising expectations among "the wretched of the earth." How ought Christians today, as individuals and through institutions, to think, speak, and act so as to respect the limitations of their situation, while yet fully exploiting its unique possibilities of human authenticity? Something like this must be the paradigmatic question of practical theology in our time, else its concern with the specifically religious and clerical will be a mere abstraction torn from its total context.

In short, the scope of theology's practical discipline is as broad as the whole of human culture, and it properly considers every form of human activity as potentially bearing the contemporary witness of faith. This is the reason its natural *Gesprächspartner* are all the human sciences and the various arts, including law, medicine, business, government, education, etc., that in any way have to do with the realization of human good.

With so broad a scope, practical theology may at first appear to lack the integrity of a single discipline. But as in the case of historical theology, there is one point toward which all its tasks converge. We have learned that theology as such is correlative in structure because it is reflective understanding of the given correlation of witness and existence. Furthermore, it should be clear that, while all three of its disciplines reflect this same correlation, each stands in a different relation to its two poles. Systematic theology is distinctive in that it reflects neither pole in itself but precisely their correlation, whereas historical theology peculiarly reflects the pole of witness, and practical theology, that of existence. Yet just as historical theology converges on critical interpretation of scripture, so practical theology is one in the way each of its different tasks is related to the other pole of existence—namely, by contributing to one comprehensive understanding of the present human situation in its limitations and possibilities. And this, of course, is just the point where practical theology is of prime importance for its sister disciplines; for it is for the sake of this situation and its authentic possibilities that all theological reflection finally exists, even as it is in its terms that all theological statements—whether historical or systematic—must somehow become credible.

It is altogether fitting, therefore, that practical theology should stand last in our consideration of the three disciplines. For with even better reason than Friedrich Schleiermacher, we, too, may say that "practical theology is the crown of theological study" (Schleiermacher, 1910).

9. *Given the differentiation of theology into its three disciplines and their still further specialization into an indefinite number of special inquiries, there arises the urgent task, essential to all disciplines and specialties alike, of fundamental theology.*

At the advanced stage of development which theology in general has now attained, the disadvantages of the division of labor whereby such development has alone become possible are not to be denied. As in other fields of understanding, the growth of specialization has tended toward a situation where individual inquirers know more and more about less and less, with a resulting fragmentation of the field and the breakdown of communication within it. Bad as such a situation may be in any case, it is disastrous in the case of theology. Encompassing though it certainly is, theology still is a single field constituted by an integral movement of reflective understanding. Consequently, given this situation, it becomes a pressing responsibility of everyone working within the field to assist in recovering its essential unity.

Yet since differentiation as such and even specialization neither can nor should be simply repealed, the only way in which this may be done is by taking up the task that is here called "fundamental theology": reflection undertaken within each of the specialties and disciplines directed toward formulating their respective first principles and thereby reestablishing communication between them. In the nature of the case, this kind of fundamental reflection, especially as it pertains to method, will seem particularly incumbent on systematic theology; and, of course, "fundamental theology" is commonly used to designate a task or specialty peculiar to the systematic discipline. But to leave the task so designated here solely in the hands of systematicians is seriously to underestimate the problem that gives rise to it. Aside from the fact that systematic theology is fully as much a part of the problem as any of the other disciplines or specialties, little is gained by a few of its specialists' projecting schemes of unity that their colleagues feel justified in ignoring for the sake of their own special inquiries. Since the problem itself is a problem of the whole field, its solution as well belongs to the field as a whole. And while this almost certainly means that a number of individuals must make it the object of their special attention, these individuals must be found within each of the three disciplines.

10. *Theological understanding as such, and thus all its disciplines and specialties as well, is in a broad sense "practical" in that, in understanding the witness of faith as decisive for human existence, it, too, is ordered to the realization of authenticity.*

Here the commentary may be brief, since this is simply the necessary conclusion of what has already been said. Although all forms of reflective understanding, even the most theoretical, are in the broadest sense "practical," in that they exist for the sake of authentic existence, they obviously differ in the ways in which they serve this final end. Thus, as compared with the special sciences—including the human sciences—such arts as law, medicine, business, or education have to do quite directly with the realization of human good. In somewhat the same way, theology, too, is as a whole "practical"; for while it is ordered not merely to some particular aspect of human good, but to the comprehensive end of authenticity as such, it nevertheless serves this end as directly as critical reflection can. The reason for this, of course, is the existential character of the witness of faith, which alone makes theological understanding either possible or necessary. Because this witness advances the claim to be decisive for human existence, theology can adequately reflect it only by sharing in the same existential finality. Accordingly, even when it is most theoretical, theology can be itself only by being just what it has traditionally been described as being: *sapientia eminens practica*.

11. *Even so, the realization of authenticity by a personal existence of "faith working through love" is in no way necessary to theological understanding, although, conversely, this kind of understanding is in a way necessary to authentic faith and love.*

If the preceding thesis affirmed the close connection of theology with the witness of faith, and thus with human existence, this one is intended to rule out an inference commonly drawn from such an affirmation. This is the inference that one of the conditions of the possibility of theological understanding is that the theologian must have already accepted the Christian witness by an existential decision of faith. One might suppose that the obvious impossibility of insisting on such a condition in the case of historical theology would have long since proved the insistence mistaken. But, unfortunately, this difficulty seems rather to have led theologians for the most part to question whether historical theology is really theology, while still insisting that the condition be met in the case of the other disciplines. Nonetheless, the whole notion of any such condition is so burdened with difficulties that not even the support of a majority can suffice to maintain it.

Thus, for one thing, it evidently makes it practically impossible for anyone to undertake the work of the theologian. If among the conditions of the possibility of my theological work is my own personal acceptance of the Christian witness, how could I or anyone else ever know when I was in a position to undertake it? By what test or tests could it be determined that I was qualified for my task? Since not even I myself can presume to look upon my heart, which God alone is able to judge, either there is no such test available to human judgment, in which case the condition of my personal faith cannot be known to be met; or else it can be known to be met, but only insofar as faith is taken to be certified by professing certain beliefs. In this case, the question arises how anyone having the least regard for the scriptural understanding of "faith" could suppose that professing even the most orthodox beliefs is any guarantee of the presence of faith either in oneself or in another. Furthermore, one must ask whether the idea of such a condition does not involve a theoretical difficulty of the first magnitude. If in order to understand the Christian witness one must first believe it, under what conditions could one ever possibly disbelieve it? After all, ignorance of the Christian claim is one thing; the express rejection of its claim by unfaith, something else. And could there ever be any such rejection until ignorance had first given way to understanding? But if an implication of the idea is that unfaith is impossible, what, then, of the distinction between unfaith and faith? Could one be meaningfully said to believe a claim that one could under no conditions be meaningfully said to disbelieve? The conclusion of this line of questioning is that faith can be made a condition of theological understanding only by making both it and any reflective understanding of it strictly impossible because neither concept any longer has coherent sense.

Yet, clearly, if so many theologians have insisted on this condition, there must be some reason for it. One suggestion is that their insistence is due to an understandable confusion about what is, in fact, a condition of theological understanding. We saw above that, like philosophy and the human sciences, theology is understanding of understanding, in that its object is the meaningful human activity of witness. Hence there is a profound sense in which theology can understand its object only by becoming it, only by permitting the object indirectly to become the subject of understanding. But if we are to avoid the sorts of difficulties just indicated, we must also recognize that what is required here is not that the theologian accept the *answer* of the witness of faith, but only that he or she ask the *question* to which it is addressed. In other words, the real condition of the possibility of one subject's understanding another is the same in theology as everywhere else—that both subjects share more or less reflectively in a common question.

What may well cause confusion in the case of theology, however, is the peculiarity of the question with which it is concerned. Since this question is the "limiting question" of human existence itself, it is logically odd—in that it is in effect self-answering, or such as to exclude the possibility of meaningful alternative answers more than verbally different from one another. Consequently, the question common to witness and theology is not sharply distinct from its answer, which may possibly account for their being confused. Understandable or not, however, a confusion is still a confusion and can and should be avoided.

And the same holds for fallacious inferences. For the other plausible suggestion as to what may account for the insistence on faith as a condition of theology is the truth of the converse relation as affirmed in the dependent clause of the present thesis. Because theology is in a way necessary to faith—namely, to its full self-understanding and adequate witness through the "works of love"—one may also be led to think that faith is somehow necessary to theology. But any such inference is formally a fallacy, and there are material reasons of the most fundamental kind why it can never be made a valid conclusion. From the standpoint of faith itself, theology can be nothing more than a form of human understanding that, for all its importance and possibility for good, falls entirely within the sphere of works. Accordingly, while faith cannot but acknowledge theology as essential to its own activity as love, it knows that the converse does not hold, any more than it holds in the case of other good works. Even though faith without theology is not really faith at all, theology without faith is still theology, and quite possibly good theology at that.

12. *For this reason, and also because theology is subject to no other criteria of truth than apply to its cognate fields generally, there can be no question of its right to exist in principle beside such other forms of reflective understanding as philosophy, the special sciences, and the various arts.*

It is a reasonable inference that typical modern doubts about the very existence of theology finally rest on two closely related suppositions: (1) that theology by its very nature involves an appeal to special criteria of truth to establish some or all of its statements; and (2) that the theologian must be a believer already committed to the Christian understanding of ultimate reality, and thus to the truth of the statements that theological reflection ostensibly seeks to establish. That these suppositions are not simply the invention of unfriendly critics but are largely justified by theology's own traditional self-understanding cannot be denied. But equally undeniable—at least to anyone sharing the basic outlook of modern secularity—is that they furnish more than sufficient reason to question theology's claim to be a legitimate form of human understanding. If theology is the kind of undertaking it is widely supposed to be—by theologians themselves as well as by their modern critics—its right to exist even in principle is far from clear.

But, obviously, the purpose of this entire discussion has been to show that there is no reason why theology has to conform to these suppositions and good reasons why it should not. Although the witness of faith that theology reflects implicitly claims to be true—indeed, to be the ultimate truth of human existence—its appeal in support of this claim is to no other conditions than those universally established with existence as such. Hence, however special theological statements may be in that they arise solely from reflection on the specifically Christian witness of faith, they are true (insofar as they are so) only because they meet the requirements of completely general criteria. Similarly, we have learned that there are the best of reasons for not supposing the personal faith of the theologian to be a necessary condition of his or her theological understanding. Not only is such a supposition implicitly self-contradictory, but it also confuses faith and works, thereby violating faith's deepest understanding of itself. In short, if the preceding argument is sound, the usual doubts about theology's right to exist pertain not to theology itself, but only to a traditional understanding of it, which can and should be overcome.

A possible objection to this conclusion is that the traditional understanding at least has the merit of preserving theology's distinctiveness, whereas the understanding developed here succeeds in meeting modern doubts only by, in effect, dissolving theology into some other form of reflection, such as the general study of religion. But the reply to this objection should be clear. Even though theology as we have come to understand it is not distinctive either in appealing to special criteria of truth or in requiring the special qualification of faith of those who would engage in it, we certainly have not concluded that there is nothing distinctive about it at all. On the contrary, we have stated more than once that theology as such would be neither possible nor necessary but for the prior reality of its object, the Christian witness of faith, with its claim to be decisive for human existence. Were it not for this witness, theological reflection would have neither object nor data; and there certainly would be no need for it without the continuing activity of witness, which calls for theological understanding as necessary to its own enablement. But because this witness itself is incontestably distinctive—even within the general field of religion—the same must also be true of theology as the single movement whereby it is alone adequately reflected. Therefore, in securing theology's right to exist, we have secured it this right precisely as theology—as a distinct form of reflection identical with none, and yet cognate with all, of the other legitimate forms of human understanding.

Of course, whether theology also has the right to exist *in fact* remains an open question, just as it does in the case of every other form of reflective understanding. And this is so for essentially the same two reasons: (1) because of all the projects that human beings may in principle undertake, only some should in fact be undertaken, given the extent of human needs and of the always limited resources for meeting them; and (2) because not every form of understanding that is in principle subject to generally applicable criteria can in fact be sustained when such criteria are applied. But if the urgency of theology and its truth are always open to question, it is significant that both forms of the question are themselves theological. At any rate, they cannot be answered at all, as distinct from being begged, except by engaging in logically the same kind of inquiry in which theology itself consists.

2

On Revelation

1

According to Rudolf Bultmann, the idea of revelation in the New Testament "contains not only the idea that our salvation rests on revelation as God's wondrous action, and only on it, so that without it we would be and remain in death, but also the idea that revelation has occurred decisively in the sending of Jesus Christ and becomes present from moment to moment in word and faith" (1930: 663–664; see also Ogden [ed.]: 58–91). On the assumption that this remains a sound, if succinct, summary of the results of contemporary exegesis, the thesis of the present study is twofold: (1) that an adequate Christian systematic theology must continue to acknowledge the necessity of revelation in two different, though closely related, senses of the word; but (2) that, for various reasons, it can no longer account for this necessity in the ways that have hitherto been typical of Christian witness and theology. The nature of the argument to be developed in support of this thesis, as well as its limitations, may be further clarified by brief comments on both parts of this initial formulation.

Although the task of systematic theology differs from that of historical theology, including exegesis, the primary test of the appropriateness of a systematic statement can only be its congruence with the witness of the apostles that is contained in the New Testament. Of course, simply to specify this test is a good deal easier than to apply it. We now recognize not only the historicity of exegesis, and the ongoing evolution in both its methods and its results, but also the irreducible pluralism of motifs as well as of forms of expression already documented by the New Testament writings themselves. In fact, we can hardly deny that "the witness of the apostles that is contained in the New Testament" is rather the object of theological interpretation than its datum and that, therefore, all attempts to test the appropriateness of systematic statements are bound to be circular. This is all the more so since it has now become clear that the apostolic witness is not simply identical with the New Testament writings, but must first be reconstructed from them before there is anything given to interpret (see below, pp. 52–57, 64–65).

But more than that, on the position taken here, appropriateness neither is nor can be the only criterion of systematic adequacy. Congruence with the apostolic witness, although a necessary test of systematic statements, is not sufficient. Insofar as such statements also claim to be true, and thus solicit the assent of every human mind, they perforce render themselves subject to the further criterion of credibility. Here, too, naturally, the test of the criterion is much more easily stated than applied. To determine whether such general criteria of truth as one must invoke to apply it are in fact what they purport to be involves one in yet another "hermeneutical circle," from which there likewise is no escape. But we need not dwell on this further difficulty, since it is only incidental to the immediate point—that congruence with the witness of the apostles is not only a difficult test to apply to systematic statements, but is also an insufficient test, since by itself it can establish nothing whatever as to their truth.

Nevertheless, the claim stands that the appropriateness of systematic statements is as necessary to their adequacy as is their credibility and that the primary test of their appropriateness is their agreement with the apostolic witness. Accordingly, any account of the meaning of "revelation" that is to be systematically adequate must pass this primary test. Although this would not suffice to establish its adequacy, failure of the test would be quite enough to establish the contrary.

As for the second part of the formulation, the pertinent comment is that systematic theology as such is, above all, precisely a matter of giving an account. If theological reflection has anything distinctive to contribute, it lies less in its conclusions than in its arguments, less in the claims it advances than in the reasons it gives for them. Correspondingly, the burden of theological reflection is always to criticize conventional accounts, thereby eliminating those that can no longer be maintained and, so far as possible, indicating others whereby the claims of the Christian witness may still be validated. From what has been said, it will be evident that the relevant accounts are of two basic kinds: those pertaining to the appropriateness of systematic statements, and thus to establishing their agreement with the witness of the apostles; and those pertaining to their credibility, and thus to validating their truth in accordance with completely general criteria, themselves critically established.

Obviously, there are severe limits to pursuing either kind of account in a single study, especially on a topic as fundamental as revelation. Consequently, the exegetical side of the present argument is not to be developed beyond indicating what I take to be a sufficiently responsible interpretation of the New Testament understanding of revelation to be worthy of serious consideration. And so, too, with the other side of the argument, which must be left even less developed. So far from trying to establish my own understanding of revelation as true, I must be content merely to formulate as clearly as I can what one would need to argue for in order to establish it.

2

The argument may appropriately begin with the first of the two ideas that Bultmann holds to be included in the New Testament idea of revelation—namely, that our salvation so entirely depends on the saving action of God that without the revelation by which this action occurs our only future would be death. I take it that there is little question that this complex idea is, in fact, an essential component of the New Testament understanding of revelation. In this understanding, not only is every human being as such utterly dependent on the prevenient action of God for his or her authentic life, but this action takes place precisely as a revelation, as a manifestation of God to a being capable of receiving and responding to such a manifestation. But if this is correct, an essential step toward a systematic account of the meaning of "revelation" is to consider just what is implied by this understanding. For, clearly, no such account could be com-

plete that failed to include what the New Testament itself necessarily presupposes in understanding revelation as it does. Our
first question, therefore, is this: What is implied as to the sense
or senses of the word "revelation" by the New Testament's own
basic presuppositions in using it?

The answer, I shall argue, is that "revelation" in one sense
of the word properly designates the original event that is constitutive not only of Christian existence but also of human existence in general or simply as such. To see the reasons for this,
consider, first, the understanding of God that the New Testament
presupposes. Despite the fact that the language in which it typically speaks of God is that either of myth or of a merely categorial metaphysics, there is abundant evidence that the God to
whom it bears witness is only inadequately represented by all
such language. When Paul confesses, for instance, that for Christians, "there is one God, the Father, from whom are all things
and for whom we exist" (1 Cor. 8:6), or, in ascribing glory to
God, attests that "from him and through him and to him are all
things" (Rom. 11:36), any merely mythical or categorial understanding of God is clearly transcended. And what we find in
Paul is documented by New Testament theology more generally.
The theism it presupposes is, in intention if not in symbol and
concept, a truly radical or transcendental theism. God is implicitly understood to be not merely one being among others,
even the greatest, but, in the phrase of the later theological tradition, "the being of all beings"—the one strictly universal individual whose individuality is constitutive of reality as such.

To this extent, the classical theistic tradition has always been
justified in insisting that the existence of God, as intended in
the New Testament, must be conceived as necessary existence.
As the ultimate ground and end of "all things," and thus of any
other existence that is so much as conceivable. God can exist
only necessarily, being the necessary condition even of the possibility of whatever comes to exist. Implied by such necessary
existence, however, is that God also is and must be strictly ubiquitous or omnipresent. Precisely as transcendent, as the one universal individual distinct from all others, God is and must be
immanent in all things as their primal source, even as they are
all immanent in God as their final end. But in this case, if anything whatever is experienced or understood, even as barely pos-

sible, God, too, must be somehow experienced or understood as its necessary source and end.

This brings us to the second reason for the answer to our question: the understanding of human existence that is also presupposed by the New Testament's uses of the word "revelation." Here, too, of course, one must insist on a distinction between the intention of New Testament anthropology and the symbols and concepts in which this intention is only imperfectly expressed. But allowing for this distinction, one may say that the human beings of which the New Testament intends to speak are beings who not only exist and experience but also understand—who do not simply live their lives in the manner of their fellow creatures but are both given and required to lead their lives by understanding themselves in relation to their world. In fact, it is just such self-understanding at its most fundamental level which, in the New Testament view, is the constitutive event of human existence. We each are or become human only because or insofar as we relate ourselves understandingly, and thus in freedom and responsibility, both to our own existence and to the world around us.

Yet this is not all. The New Testament expressly affirms that simply as human beings we are also understandingly related to God, if only in the inauthentic mode of misunderstanding God's gift and demand, and regardless of the extent to which such understanding as we have is adequately reflected upon and expressed. So, according to the Prologue to the Fourth Gospel, the Word that was in the beginning with God, and was God, was also the source of life and as such "the light of men," indeed, "the true light that enlightens every man" (Jn. 1:1, 4, 9). Or again, Paul insists that all men are "without excuse" for their ingratitude and idolatry, since "what can be known about God is plain to them, because God has manifested it to them" (Rom. 1:19–20). Or finally, there is the speech in Acts 17:23–28, in which Paul is represented as saying to the Athenians, "What therefore you worship as unknown, this I proclaim to you. The God who made the world and everything in it . . . made from one every nation of men to live on all the face of the earth, having determined allotted periods and the boundaries of their habitation, that they should seek God, and perchance might feel after him and find him, though he is not far from each one of us; for 'In him we live and move and are.' "

Recalling the understanding of God that the New Testament presupposes, we should have no difficulty seeing the reason for these typical affirmations. If God does and must exist necessarily, and thus must somehow be understood if anything at all is understood, the constitutive event of human existence as the event of self-understanding can only include an understanding of God. We each are or become human only because or insofar as, in understanding ourselves and our world, we also relate ourselves understandingly to the gift and demand of God's love. Consequently, whatever the New Testament's own uses of "revelation," there can be no question that, given the presuppositions of its uses with respect to human existence as well as to God, God is and must be present to every human being simply as such in the event in which, being present to ourselves and our world, we are each also present to God.

Of course, the New Testament itself speaks of this original presentation of God to us precisely as "revelation." This is evident, for example, from the fact, uniformly obscured in the commonly used translations, that Paul uses the very same verb φανερόω in Rom 1:19, "What can be known about God is plain to them because God has manifested [=ἐφανέρωσεν] it to them," that he uses in Rom. 3:21, "But now the righteousness of God has been manifested [=πεφανέρωται] apart from the law, although the law and the prophets bear witness to it, the righteousness of God through faith in Jesus Christ for all who believe." But important as it is to recognize this, the argument I have developed is not just from some particular New Testament uses of "revelation," but from what is necessarily presupposed by *all* its uses—namely, that the only God who is revealed to us is such as to be universally understood and that the only human existence that is the recipient of God's revelation is such that it can and must understand this God. The value of this argument, I believe, is to disclose the deeper reasons for the New Testament's own speaking of revelation as in one sense universal because it is the original event of every human life. So far from merely reflecting the then current apologetic situation (as shaped, say, by Hellenistic Judaism or Stoic natural theology), such speaking was the necessary implication of the understanding of God and human existence that was fundamental to the entire New Testament witness.

If this is correct, however, there also is no great difficulty in accounting for the appropriateness of theology's characteristic acknowledgment throughout most of its long history of something like a "natural revelation"—or, as I prefer to say, following Friedrich Schleiermacher, "original revelation" (1960: 1: 30). The warrant for such acknowledgment, including the teaching of the First Vatican Council that "God, the beginning and end of all things, can be certainly known by the natural light of human reason from created things," is by no means only that the New Testament itself expressly makes it but that it is also strictly entailed by the New Testament's most fundamental presuppositions concerning human existence and God (Denzinger: 588).

On the other hand, the criticism to be made of the relatively few theologies that have simply denied original revelation is not merely that it is a strange kind of loyalty to scripture to deny for its sake what it itself plainly affirms, as Emil Brunner rightly urged in his famous controversy with Karl Barth (Brunner: 12). The more serious criticism is that any such denial, however unintentionally, is in the way of denying one or the other of the New Testament's own most basic presuppositions. If the argument I have developed is sound, the denial of original revelation necessarily entails the following dilemma: either God is not really God in the New Testament understanding of the term, or human existence is not human existence according to the same understanding. Thus when Barth, in utterly denying original revelation, nevertheless allowed that "man is man and not a cat," he was by implication denying that God is the God to whom the New Testament intends to bear witness (Barth: 25).

3

Yet if there are the best of reasons for acknowledging that revelation in one sense of the word is the original presentation of God to every human understanding, clearly this is not the only, or even the primary, sense of "revelation" in the New Testament. As Bultmann rightly emphasizes, what the New Testament itself says about revelation includes the further idea that it has occurred decisively in the special event of Jesus Christ, and that it takes place again and again in the present in the witness and faith of which this event is the principle as well as the origin. Consequently, from the New Testament down to our own time, the primary sense of "revelation" in Christian theology has not been "original revelation" but what I call "special revelation," and, more exactly, "decisive revelation," which is to say, the re-presentation of God that has taken place and continues to take place through the particular strand of human history of which Jesus is the center. So true is this, in fact, that even theologians who have acknowledged that revelation is in some sense universal have usually intended something very different from the original revelation that I find it imperative to acknowledge.

Thus while Paul Tillich, for instance, expressly speaks of "universal revelation," he characteristically asserts or implies that special revelation of some sort or other is the only revelation there is. This is evident from his analysis of revelation as the self-manifestation of ultimate mystery in a special miraculous event received in an ecstatic experience. "Mystery," "miracle," and "ecstasy"—these, according to Tillich, are the essential marks of revelation; and from this it follows that one properly speaks of revelation only insofar as one can also speak of a "medium" (or "bearer") of revelation in the form of some natural or historical event accompanied by human language. But this is to say, in effect, that one can speak only of special revelation; and so Tillich is only consistent when he takes "universal revelation" to refer not even to the universal occurrence of special revelation but only to its occurrence well beyond the bounds of "final revelation" and to the "universal possibility" of its occurrence (1951: 106–159, espec. 138–142).

The point of this reference to Tillich is not to criticize but simply to underscore that it is precisely the sense of revelation as special revelation, or decisive revelation, by which the usual systematic treatments of the topic are all determined, including even revisionary ones such as his. To employ the distinction used in recent Roman Catholic theology, I could say that what is generally meant by "revelation" in theological treatises is not "transcendental revelation" but "categorial (or predicamental) revelation" (Rahner and Ratzinger: 11–24; see also Lonergan: 119). It is the revelation constitutive of all specifically Christian existence, as distinct from human existence in general or simply as such.

The further and more important point, however, is that Christian theology has universally claimed that revelation in this sense is necessary. Even where the necessity of original revelation has been disputed or obscured, special revelation has not only consistently been acknowledged but acknowledged as something that simply had and has to take place. One reason for this, obviously, is that, being constitutive of all Christian faith and witness, as well as of their theological interpretation, the representation of God in Jesus Christ has to be acknowledged as a *sine qua non* because it is the strictly necessary condition of the possibility of Christian existence as such. But it is just as obvious that this minimal necessity is by no means the only necessity that theologians have typically claimed for special revelation, even if such other reasons as they have given for their claim are open to serious objections. The second question we need to ask, therefore, is how this traditional claim is to be accounted for. By what reasons, if any, can we continue to acknowledge not only that God is revealed decisively in Jesus Christ but also that this revelation is necessary?

One type of answer that we can no longer accept, I believe, might be developed as follows: Granted that there is, indeed, an original revelation of God to every human understanding, this revelation, being purely "natural," is in no way self-sufficient. Since, on any account, there is more to revelation and authentic faith in God than merely understanding that and what God is— even with full reflectiveness—all "natural revelation" as well as all "natural theology" does and must point beyond itself. Seeing, then, that the more to which it points is just what is manifested in the particular history of which Jesus is the center, we both may and must affirm that this history constitutes a properly "supernatural" revelation that is revelation in a special—indeed decisive—sense.

This, I take it, is the kind of answer to our question that would most likely be given to it by anyone oriented to the great central tradition of Christian theology. In the particular form it has received from the representatives of orthodoxy, Protestant and Catholic alike, it is characterized not only by the systematic distinction between "nature and grace," "the natural and the supernatural," but also by the tacit assumption that revelation and faith are primarily a matter of acquiring knowledge. Thus special revelation is held to be necessary, in the last analysis, because it is only through it that the distinctive truths of Christianity, or the "mysteries of faith," are so represented to the human intellect as to be even possibly the objects of its attention and belief.

The decisive objection to this orthodox form of the answer is that the New Testament itself in no way warrants the assumption that God's revelation in Jesus Christ consists primarily in communicating supernatural knowledge. Although there are passages in the New Testament, just as in the Old, where revelation is indeed spoken of in some such way, scripture does not characteristically appeal to revelation as providing special knowledge of God's existence and nature. This is sufficiently evident from the fact, rightly stressed by Bultmann, that it is entirely innocent of any particular theological problem in somehow relating what we know through revelation to our natural and rational knowledge (1930: 661). But there is no need to labor the objection, what with the consensus that has now come to exist that orthodoxy's distinctive understanding of revelation can no longer claim the sanction of the New Testament. Not only Protestant neo-orthodoxy but, increasingly, progressive Roman Catholic theology as well, provides abundant evidence that any understanding of revelation as primarily the communication of supernatural knowledge has now been overcome (Baillie; Baum: 43).

It would be wrong to suppose, however, that the same is true of the understanding of special revelation as in a proper sense supernatural. Despite their abandonment of the notion that such revelation itself consists in supernatural truths, most theologians continue to think and speak of it as a supernatural occurrence which grounds a knowledge of God and ourselves beyond any that nature and reason as such could provide. In fact, stressing, as they do, that, on the New Testament idea of revelation as event, it is God's wondrous act of salvation, they find more than sufficient reason to insist on its character precisely as supernatural. But there are also serious objections to this modified understanding, insofar as it is taken to answer our question as to the reasons for affirming the necessity of special revelation.

This is especially so of the form of the understanding which has recently been worked out by progressive Catholic theologians. Not the least motive of their work has been to see to it that the problem of revelation as it was acutely posed by the Catholic modernists is at last given a more adequate solution than any previously available in the official teaching and theology of the church (Rahner and Ratzinger: 11–13; Baum: 44). Thus while they have been careful, as the modernists were not, to maintain the distinction between nature and grace, the natural and the supernatural, they have also made the point that strictly supernatural grace and, therefore, revelation are themselves constitutive of every human existence. Karl Rahner makes this point in his quasi-Heideggerian way by arguing that grace and revelation (specifically, "transcendental revelation") are a "supernatural existential": as supernatural, they must be referred to a second, strictly gratuitous act of God's love in addition to that of creation, even though as existential they are also a constitutive factor of human existence as such. But the objection to this kind of an understanding is that it by no means makes clear why God's special revelation in Jesus Christ should be necessary. Even if there is a more to revelation and faith that is strictly supernatural, if this more belongs, or, in the case of faith, *can* belong, to human existence quite apart from Christian revelation, it can hardly serve to explain the necessity of this revelation.

Rahner himself, of course, is sensitive to this objection and usually tries to meet it by arguing that the grace and revelation given to every human being transcendentally are precisely and only the grace and revelation of Christ's incarnation, on which they are entirely dependent as on their final end. But one hardly knows what to make of this argument, seeing that Rahner is just as emphatic that the mystery of the incarnation itself has its ultimate ground and end in the *Urgeheimnis* of God's decision to communicate Godself in love to every human being. Considering that, in Rahner's view, all the *mysteria stricte dicta* of trinity, incarnation, and grace are revealed implicitly in every person's encounter with this primal mystery, we have ample reason to conclude that the only sense, finally, in which he can consistently claim that specifically Christian revelation is necessary is in whatever sense this may be claimed for the full and adequate explication of this primal encounter.

Even if Catholic theologians could consistently claim more than this, however, they would still be faced with a more serious objection which also applies to the understanding typical of much Protestant neo-orthodoxy. This is the objection that the whole distinction between nature and grace, the natural and the supernatural, must be regarded with profound suspicion from the standpoint of the New Testament as well as of scripture generally. To some extent, of course, Protestant theology has always been critical of this distinction as understood and employed by Catholic theologians. Lutheran and Reformed orthodoxy alike rejected the doctrine that "original righteousness" is a *donum superadditum*, on the ground that its implication that our natural state was imperfect clearly conflicts with Gen. 1:31 (Schmid: 158; Heppe: 190–191). And yet their own understanding that God's original gifts to human beings were natural did not preclude speaking of God's revelation in Jesus Christ as supernatural. For even these natural gifts themselves must be called supernatural, insofar as they are "above the nature *corrupted by sin* and are not restored except by supernatural grace" (Heppe: 191). Consistent with this traditional Protestant position, then, neo-orthodox theologians who have acknowledged something like a "natural revelation" have continued to think in terms of the distinction between "nature and grace." This is most obvious in the case of Brunner, whose use of the distinction is explicit; but a somewhat similar, if significantly qualified, position is also taken by Reinhold Niebuhr in his Gifford Lectures (R. Niebuhr: 1: 125–149; cf. 2: 109, n. 6, 123, 208).

Although, on this position, revelation itself is by no means the communication of supernatural truths, something more is revealed in Christ than is revealed to human existence originally or "naturally." In formal terms, this more is typically conceived by analogy with our knowledge of another human person. We do not really come to know a woman herself, say, as distinct from merely knowing about her, until she interprets herself to us through her own personal word. But this strictly formal conception is characteristically entangled with the claim that there is also a difference in content between all that we can know of God naturally or rationally and what is made known to us in Christ alone. While natural revelation may indeed confront us with the God of power and law, thereby establishing our responsibility, it is solely in Christ that we meet the God of love and grace and thus can live by faith and no longer merely by works.

But it is just this claim that special revelation has a different content from original revelation that the New Testament sharply calls into question. This is sufficiently evident from the reflection that, since a merely partial divine revelation can at most establish a merely partial human responsibility, it cannot possibly be what Paul intends to assert in Romans 1:18–20. And what does he mean there by the "power" of God, which he asserts that God has manifested to everyone, if not the very thing of which he speaks when he says in a preceding verse that the gospel is "the power of God for salvation to everyone who has faith, to the Jew first and also to the Greek" (vs. 16), or witnesses elsewhere that "Christ crucified" is precisely "Christ the power of God and the wisdom of God" (1 Cor. 1:23–24)?

The answer, I believe, is clear and, together with all the other evidence that Bultmann has carefully reviewed, fully justifies the conclusion he draws from it: "There is no other light shining in Jesus than has always already shined in the creation. Man learns to understand himself in the light of the revelation of redemption no differently than he always already should understand himself in face of the revelation in creation and the law—namely, as God's creature who is limited by God and stands under God's claim, which opens up to him the way to death or to life. If the revelation in Jesus means salvation as an understanding of oneself in him, then the revelation in creation meant nothing other than this understanding of oneself in God in the knowledge of one's own creatureliness" (Ogden [ed.]: 86).

Furthermore, in the systematic aspect of his work, Bultmann develops an alternative account of the distinctive "more" of revelation and faith beyond such knowledge of the existence and nature of God as is originally available to human existence. Appealing to the analogy of human friendship, he argues that the more I come to know when I actually find a friend is "nothing more *about* friendship," but simply that "I now know my friend and also know myself anew, in the sense that, in understanding my friend, my concrete life in its work and its joy, its struggle and its pain, is qualified in a new way. In knowing my friend in the *event* of friendship, the events of my life become new—

'new' in a sense that is valid only for me and visible only to me, that indeed only *becomes* visible in the now and thus must always become visible *anew*" (Ogden [ed.]: 99–100).

By means of this analogy, conceptually clarified by Martin Heidegger's distinction between *Existenzialität* and *Existenz*, Bultmann interprets the more of special revelation and faith as precisely their event—as consisting, therefore, not in *what* is revealed and believed in but in the fact *that* revelation and faith take place in my own existence. Thus he shows how the traditional distinction between nature and grace not only should but can be dispensed with, even while acknowledging that there is indeed more to revelation and authentic faith than what we can originally know of the nature and existence of God. "The revelation of God brings no knowledge about the mysteries of other worlds; in fact, it communicates nothing even about God that any reflective person could not know by himself—namely, that man can receive his life by God's grace only in radical solitariness before him. No revelation needs to tell me what God's grace *means*. One thing alone it tells me, and with that it tells me everything: 'This grace holds good for *thee*!' and because it tells me this in the words, 'Thy sin is forgiven thee!' it opens my eyes to the fact that the first and last sin of man is to want to be himself by his own power" (Bultmann, 1952: 272).

And yet, as is well known, Bultmann himself takes the position that God's decisive revelation in Christ is necessary not only to Christian existence but also to any human existence that is to actualize its authentic possibility. This is so, Bultmann argues, because, in spite of God's original revelation to human beings in the understanding of their own creatureliness, they do not really understand themselves as creatures and thereby honor and give thanks to their Creator. Their response to God's revelation is not the authentic response of faith but rather the inauthentic response of sin—the attempt to secure the ultimate meaning of their existence by what they themselves are and have and do, instead of living, finally, by God's grace alone. So while it is indeed necessary to acknowledge original revelation, it is also necessary to speak of it as now lying in the past, as something that, as men and women actually exist in the present, they have quite forgotten or suppressed. Having thus already lost their authentic possibility, then, they can have no hope of actualizing it unless God acts preveniently to restore it to them. But since it is just this that God has in fact done in sending Jesus Christ and establishing the Christian proclamation, it is this event as it takes place ever anew through word and sacraments that is God's decisive revelation not only to Christians but to all humankind.

This answer to our question is clearly different from any of the family of answers we have considered. It also seems clear, to me at least, that it is notably more appropriate to the underlying intention of the New Testament witness. Yet even to it there are sufficiently serious objections that it cannot be accepted just as it is.

The crux of these objections can be brought out by relying on a line of reasoning similar to that by which Catholic theologians such as Rahner attempt to show that supernatural grace and revelation are constitutive of every human existence, and that this is a fact whether or not one explicitly knows it and regardless of one's acceptance of specifically Christian revelation. The ground of this fact, these theologians argue, is God's will that human beings universally shall be saved, which follows from God's primal decision to communicate Godself in love, which already lies behind (although it need not have lain behind) God's creation of the world. Because God has graciously decided to be the final end of all things, God wills to be present and, in fact, is present to every human being, so that even in the state of sin none of us is ever without the possibility of authentic faith.

But now, like any deduction, this reasoning can be reversed, with the following significant result: if any human being is ever simply without the possibility of authentic faith, even if he or she has already forfeited it by his or her own sin, then God either does not will the authenticity of every human being or else is powerless to make it possible. In short, by this reasoning, the implication of Bultmann's position is that God is *not* the God who "desires all men to be saved and to come to the knowledge of the truth" nor "the living God, who is the Savior of all men, especially of those who believe" (1 Tim. 2:4, 4:10).

That this reasoning in no way depends on the distinctive premises of the Catholic version of classical Christian theism should be clear enough. But what may well be emphasized is that it is, if anything, even more to the point, given Bultmann's own very different premises. He himself expressly allows that one can support the view that "God does not exist without the world, the Creator without the creation" by appealing to John 1:1–3—"to the remarkable statement that in the beginning was the Word, the Word of the Creator, through which everything has come to be. This is the Word which was in the beginning with God, indeed, was God" (Bultmann, 1965: 125). But, then, as we have seen, Bultmann also rejects the Catholic understanding of the "double gratuity" according to which grace, properly speaking, is due to a strictly supernatural act of God above and beyond God's love in creation. Consequently, on Bultmann's own premises, creation and redemption alike must be said to be natural to God in the sense that God neither would nor could be who God essentially is were God not freely to create worlds and freely to redeem them in love. To say this, however, is to have even less reason to maintain that any human being could ever be without the possibility of authentic faith—so far, at least, as having this possibility is dependent on the action of God. On the other hand, to maintain that anyone is in fact without the possibility of faith is even more obviously to call into question either God's goodness or God's power.

Nor can this form of the problem of evil be in the least dealt with along the lines of the so-called free-will defense. To be sure, the actualization of authenticity can occur only through one's own free decision, which, in Bultmann's view, certainly does not follow necessarily from God's grace. Even God's revelation in Christ restores only the *possibility* of authentic faith, thereby leaving open the possibility of one's either continuing in sin or relapsing into it. Likewise, the extent to which one objectifies one's existence and becomes explicitly conscious of one's possibilities is also a function of human freedom, and thus a historical variable whose values include everything from ignorance and falsehood to the knowledge and truth that are given us in Jesus and in the particular history of which he is the center. But what is at issue here is neither the actualization of one's authenticity nor its full and adequate objectification—both of which clearly are dependent, in part, on one's own free choice—but rather the possibility of authentic faith, and it only insofar as it depends

on the prevenient action of God. In the nature of the case, therefore, any appeal to one's freedom and one's misuse of it is simply irrelevant to the problem and cannot even begin to solve it.

I conclude, therefore, that the dilemma that Bultmann's position involves is inescapable. Either God is not after all who
God is assumed to be, or else there is no human being who is
ever simply without God's saving grace, and hence without the
possibility of authentic faith. To hold, however, as I do, that it
is the second alternative alone that is appropriate to the apostolic
witness does not imply that there is no sense at all in which a
human being might be said to have no authentic possibility.
There are, in fact, three senses in which this might be said: (1)
in the sense that the human being in question is either not yet
or no longer a human being in the relevant meaning of the
words; (2) in the sense that, although he or she is a human
being, and thus has the possibility of authentic faith, he or she
nevertheless is not explicitly aware of having it, and so has it
only implicitly; or (3) in the sense that, although he or she is in
fact always given this possibility by God in the gift of being human, he or she not only has forfeited it in the past by his or her
own decision for inauthenticity but, despite God's unceasing re-
newal of the gift, is also presently engaged in forfeiting it (Kierkegaard: 18–19).

And yet it should already be clear from this why accepting
the second alternative entails neither a superficial understanding
of sin nor a simple identification of faith with theistic belief. One
may conceive sin as radically as one pleases, and this alternative
may still be accepted, provided only that one conceives grace as
well in a radical way. And so, too, one may say that authentic
faith in God is indeed more than explicit belief in God, even
while insisting that it is and remains every human being's possibility. For Bultmann's own insistence still stands that faith is
by no means merely a human capacity or disposition that may
be more or less fully developed. In fact, faith is not possible at
all but for the prevenient action of God, and it never becomes
actual except as event—as one's ever-new response in the moment to God's ever-new act of grace.

But if even the second answer to our question can no longer
be fully accepted, how are we to answer it? Can no reason be
given for the necessity of Christian revelation beyond the min-

imal necessity that, as we noted at the outset, can obviously be claimed for it? Is the conclusion to which we are led simply that God's revelation in Jesus Christ is indeed necessary to Christian existence but on no account necessary to human existence as such?

As this question is usually understood, the only answer, I believe, must be affirmative. I am convinced that none of the accounts of Christian revelation as necessary even to the possibility of human authenticity can continue to be maintained—and this, not because they all fail to meet certain criteria of truth but because, as I have tried to indicate, they do not pass the primary test of agreeing with the apostolic witness contained in the New Testament. Precisely when one takes the claims of this witness in the full length and breadth of their intended meaning, one is led to conclude that the only necessary, but also sufficient, condition of the possibility of authentic faith is the original self-presentation of God that is the constitutive event of all human existence and that, therefore, never fails to take place as soon and as long as there is any distinctively human being at all.

But if the conventional accounts of revelation are thereby eliminated as untenable, it may be that the usual understanding of our question is not the only way of understanding it. Perhaps if we can ask it in a different way, more can be claimed concerning the necessity of special revelation, and hence of decisive revelation, than we have so far found reason to claim.

That this is possible does, in fact, seem to be the case. Granted that original revelation, and thus the possibility of authentic faith, is constitutive of every human existence as such, it by no means follows that human beings universally are explicitly aware of this fact and all that it involves with full and adequate consciousness. As we observed earlier, the extent to which one objectifies one's existence by means of explicit concepts and symbols is a function of human freedom, both one's own and that of one's fellows, and thus is a historical variable allowing for an indefinite range of possible values.

To be sure, the apparent universality of religion in some form throughout all human culture is evidence that human beings generally have somehow understood reflectively as well as existentially the gift and demand of God's original self-presentation to their existence. In becoming acculturated within a particular tradition, individuals have normally also been formed religiously by learning to objectify the ultimate mystery of their existence in traditional concepts and symbols. But the wide variety of religious forms, of beliefs, rites, and social organizations, leaves no question that human beings are naturally religious only in something like the sense in which they are naturally social or moral. Such religion as they have, as distinct from the faith of which it is the objectification, is not natural but historical, and so is available to them only as one religion among others, as one more or less adequate response to God's original revelation.

Both facts, however—the variety and the universality of religion—attest to the existence also of special revelation and to an urgent human need for it. At the base of every religion, as its origin and principle, is some particular occasion of insight, of reflective grasp through concept and symbol, of the mystery manifested in original revelation. Thus not only Christianity but all religions exist only on the basis of, and themselves serve to constitute, some event of special revelation, which as the objectification of our existence as gift and demand claims to be decisive for it. Nor is there any difficulty in seeing the reasons for this claim. In this matter, as in all others, we cannot merely live our lives but have to lead them as well, and to this end we need to lay hold of an understanding of ourselves and of the reality encompassing us in explicit thought and speech. Even our understanding of ourselves before God is a reflective as well as an existential problem, since it is only insofar as it is fully and adequately objectified that we can become completely clear and certain as to God's gift and demand. Consequently, insofar as the God who is presented to us in all our experience and understanding is also re-presented to us through explicit concepts and symbols, we are confronted with a special revelation that may indeed claim to be decisive for our existence.

Moreover, in the religious sphere even more than in others, the problem of truth either is or becomes acute. Aside from the fact that the object of reflection here is in the nature of the case unique, and thus only improperly objectified by all our ordinary concepts and symbols, there are any number of ways in which it can be reflected, depending upon the particular aspect of human existence that is taken as focusing the problem of faith. There is also the fact that in this sphere, above all, our attempts at objectifying our experience are defeated in various ways by that inauthentic understanding of ourselves which is sin. Inevitably, then, there is the wide variety of religious insights and traditions, each with its claim to be true. But this only intensifies our need for a special revelation of God's gift and demand that will be decisive—that will objectify our existence in a full and adequate way and thereby guide our decision amidst all the claims and counterclaims to religious truth.

It is along these rather different lines, I suggest, that our question as to the necessity of Christian revelation can very well be asked. Although such revelation cannot be necessary to the *constitution* of human existence, it can very well be necessary to the *objectification* of existence, in the sense of its full and adequate understanding at the level of explicit thought and speech. Insofar, then, as such objectification is in turn necessary, if not to our being human, then to our becoming such, it is by no means only Christians for whom the re-presentation of God in Jesus Christ can in a sense be claimed to be necessary. Of course, the qualification is essential, since Christian revelation is necessary to human existence in a sense different from original revelation. Whereas original revelation, we may say, is *immediately* and *proximately* necessary to our authenticity, decisive revelation is only *mediately* and *remotely* necessary to it, being necessary in the first instance not to the constitution of our possiblity, but to its full and adequate explication (cf. Wesley: 2: 451–452, 456–457). Even so, if we need, as we do, just such an explication, we also have need of God's revelation in Jesus Christ—and this simply as human beings, quite apart from a decision for specifically Christian existence.

This can be claimed, naturally, only on the assumption that Christian revelation is, in fact, what it purports to be—namely, the full and adequate objectification of human existence in its authentic possibility. But if this assumption is true, the necessity that can be claimed for this revelation is more than a merely minimal necessity. For it is human beings as such, not merely Christians, who can live only by the word—the inner word of God's love in the depth of our existence and, therefore, the outer word in our history that is the veritable incarnation of this love.

4

There remains the task of responding to an objection that will almost certainly be made to this argument. On the understand-

ing of revelation that I have been indicating, the special revelation affirmed to be decisive by the Christian witness of faith
is simply the full and adequate explication of God's original revelation to human existence. Thus, whatever may be claimed concerning the necessity of this special revelation, it can in no way
be necessary to the very possibility of human authenticity. Not
only is there no other light shining in Jesus than has always
already shined in the creation, but no saving act of God occurs
in him other than that which never fails to occur as soon and
as long as there is any distinctively human being. If this is what
the understanding comes to, however, there are those who will
see it simply as falling back on what Kierkegaard spoke of as
"the Socratic point of view," according to which Christian revelation can be nothing more than an occasion of "recollection"
(ἀνάμνησις). Our third and final question, therefore, is whether
this is in fact the case. Does decisive revelation function merely
as a midwife at the birth in time of the eternal truths of theism,
or does it reveal something new?

We may observe, to begin with, that Kierkegaard's formulation of the alternatives in this connection is on the face of it
inexhaustive (cf. Pregeant: 8–10). As he presents them, there are
two basically different understandings of existence between
which one must choose: the Socratic understanding, according
to which *no* event is constitutive of our authentic possibility, because we already possess it implicitly prior to any event; and
Kierkegaard's own understanding, according to which *some*
event is thus constitutive, because it is in it alone that we are
given the possibility that we do not already possess, not even
implicitly. But these, obviously, are not the only alternatives logically allowed for by the very disjunction on which Kierkegaard
relies. There remains, if only as "a project of thought," a third
understanding, according to which *every* event is constitutive of
our possibility, because, while it is in no way our eternal possession, it is given to us at least implicitly in every event that is
constitutive of our existence.

There are good reasons, naturally, why Kierkegaard should
have neglected this third alternative. Like many others, he was
bent on so accounting for Christian revelation that it could be
claimed to be necessary even to the possibility of human authenticity, in that, as he himself put it, our "eternal happiness"

is based upon "historical knowledge." Nevertheless, since his understanding of existence is clearly not the only way in which one might make "an advance upon Socrates," rejection of his understanding need in no way be a retreat to "the Socratic point of view."

The pertinence of this observation, of course, is that it is the very alternative Kierkegaard neglected that has been pursued in the present argument. According to the understanding I have tried to indicate, Christian revelation is by no means merely the explication of the eternal truths of theism. While it is indeed nothing other than the full and adequate objectification of original revelation, original revelation itself is always and only an event—an event occurring in time, and so nothing merely eternal. To be sure, original revelation is not simply one event among others but, rather, the unique event which, being constitutive of human existence, always occurs insofar as we exist at all. It is the event in which God's ever-new self-presentation to the world in love not only takes place but is also received and somehow responded to understandingly as gift and demand.

To this extent, then, we do indeed possess, if only implicitly, certain eternal truths of which Christian revelation is merely the explication—such truths as that God exists and is a loving God and therefore so acts toward the world as ever and again to embrace it in love. As we noted earlier in the argument, however, there is more to revelation than our possession of such truths, even in the form of explicit belief. Original revelation itself is precisely event—the event of God's self-presentation in every moment not only as God but as *my God*, as the concrete source and end of my own unique existence and of just this particular world of which I am here and now a part. Because this is so, however, decisive revelation by no means functions merely as a midwife at the birth of explicit theism. As the objectification of God's original revelation, it is the re-presentation of God's love itself as the ever-new gift and demand of my existence.

In sum: *what* Christian revelation reveals to us is nothing new, since such truths as it makes explicit must already be known to us implicitly in every moment of our existence. But *that* this revelation occurs does reveal something new to us in that, as itself event, it is the occurrence in our history of the transcendent event of God's love. As Bultmann says of the proclamation of

Jesus, "*what* he says he does not say as anything new or unheard of; but *that* he says it, that he says it *now*, is what is decisive and what makes the situation of all who hear it into a new and decisive situation" (Bultmann, 1954: 204). This is not to say, naturally, that the content of Christian revelation is somehow unimportant or unnecessary. It is to say simply that what makes it revelation is also the fact of its occurrence and that it is with respect to this fact that it is the decisive revelation of something new: God's "new creation" in Christ, and so our own authentic possibility of "faith working through love" (2 Cor. 5:17; Gal. 6:15, 5:6).

3

The Authority of Scripture
for Theology

In what sense, if any, is the canon of scripture the sole primary authority for Christian theology?

Presupposed in asking this question is an understanding of the present theological situation as determined by two salient facts. First of all, from its beginnings in the Reformation right up to the present, Protestant theology has characteristically maintained the so-called scriptural principle. According to this principle, scripture alone is or ought to be the primary authority not only for Christian faith and witness but also for the fully reflective understanding thereof which is Christian theology. To be sure, this principle has been variously understood by Protestant theologians as they have tried to come to terms with the new limitations and opportunities of successive theological situations. But until quite recently, the vast majority of them have recognized at least some sense in which the scriptural principle can and should be maintained. The second salient fact, however, is the uncertainty expressed in recent years by a growing number of Protestant theologians whether there is any sense at all in which this principle is still tenable—or, at least, whether it can still be maintained in any of the senses in which it has heretofore been understood. The causes of this development are complex, and it is not essential to our purpose to go into them. Certainly, the growing dialogue with Roman Catholic theology has been an important factor, and continuing developments in the historical-critical understanding of scripture, even more so.

Also, in reacting in general against neo-orthodoxy by taking up once again the apologetic task of theology, Protestant theologians from the 1960s on have become increasingly critical of what James Barr has called "the modern revival of biblical authority" (Barr: 5). Not even the highly qualified senses in which neo-orthodox theologians have typically understood the scriptural principle warrant the certainty that it can still be maintained.

The question I am asking, then, would seem to have become an urgent theological question for anyone concerned with the topic of this study. But urgent or not, it is without doubt important. The scriptural principle has been so characteristic of Protestant theology throughout its history that no systematic theology today can fail to ask whether there is some sense in which the principle is still tenable. And this may be insisted on the more confidently not only because Roman Catholic theology still characteristically rejects the principle, or accepts it in a sense unacceptable to most Protestants, but also because, as I have indicated, Protestant theologians themselves have understood it in various senses which call for theological clarification and decision. Essential to the prolegomena of any contemporary theology is some answer to the question before us.

Just because the question is important, however, there are severe limits to answering it adequately in a short study. The most I can hope to do is to consider some of the basic issues that the question involves and, in so doing, sketch the broad outlines of a possible position on the topic. If I am right, there is no sense, finally, in which the canon of scripture is the sole primary authority for Christian theology any more than for Christian faith and witness. But why I believe this and what it both does and does not imply concerning the theological understanding and use of scripture I cannot explain even inadequately except by the whole of the following argument.

1. The Necessary Limit to Scripture as a Theological Authority

Most discussions of our question have proceeded on the assumption that to determine what is or is not a theological authority is *eo ipso* to determine what is or is not a sufficient authorization for the truth of theological assertions. Thus it is commonly inferred that if scripture is in any sense the sole primary authority for Christian theology, scripture is also in some sense the sole sufficient authorization that the claims of Christian theology are true. My contention, however, is that this assumption is unfounded and that the common inference concerning scripture as a theological authority must be rejected.

In the nature of the case, no authority, properly so-called, can be a sufficient authorization for the truth of the assertions derived from it or warranted by it. Unless the assertions made by the authority are themselves already authorized as true by some method other than an appeal to authority, no assertion derived from them or warranted by them can by that fact alone be an authorized assertion. This is not to deny, of course, that an assertion authorized by appeal to authority may very well be true. The point is simply that, if it is so, the fact that it is authorized by authority is not itself sufficient to make it so. Moreover, I am not in the least disputing that appeal to authority is a common and, as far as it goes, entirely legitimate method of fixing belief. But belief in an assertion is one thing, the truth of the assertion, something else; and this difference is such that logically and, therefore, necessarily no assertion that is believed on authority can be authorized by that fact alone as worthy of belief.

By the sheer logic of the case, then, there is a necessary limit to any theological authority, and hence also to scripture as a theological authority. Even if there is some sense in which scripture is the sole primary authority for theology's assertions, there neither is nor could be any sense in which it is the sole sufficient authorization that these assertions are true. I put the point in this way to obviate the misunderstanding that the limit on which I am insisting is some merely factual limit. My present contention is in no way that the authority of scripture is a limited authority, in the sense that it could be conceived to be greater than it in fact is. Whether, or in what sense, this also is true may be deferred for consideration until later in the argument. My only point now is that there is a necessary limit to any theological authority, and hence also to scripture, in that, logically or in principle, it cannot be a sufficient authorization for the truth of theological assertions. Insofar, then, as it belongs to the very nature of Christian theology as a process of reflective understanding or inquiry to see that its assertions are true, it cannot be in this essential respect that scripture is its sole primary authority.

This leads to the conclusion that further discussion of our question is pointless unless it is recognized that the authority of scripture for theology can at most be its authority with respect to but one of the ends that theological reflection is bound to pursue. Properly understood, the task of Christian theology is the fully reflective understanding of the Christian witness of faith as decisive for human existence. Consequently, to accomplish this task, theological reflection is required to pursue two essential ends: (1) to see to the appropriateness of its assertions, in the sense of their congruence in meaning with the Christian witness of faith itself; and (2) to see to the credibility of its assertions, in the sense of their truth in terms of the conditions established with existence as such. Since for the reasons I have just given scripture cannot conceivably be a sufficient authorization for the truth of theological assertions, such authority as it can have for theology cannot be with respect to securing the credibility of theology's assertions. If it is a theological authority at all, it is so only with respect to determining the appropriateness of such assertions.

In this connection, it may not be entirely misleading to recall a somewhat similar point that was made by the older orthodoxy concerning the "perfection" of scripture. This perfection, it was claimed, is a *perfectio respectu finis*, a perfection with respect to the end of human salvation, and so to witnessing to all that is necessary to the attainment of this end. By analogy with this claim, we may say that the authority of scripture, also, can only be an *auctoritas respectu finis*, an authority with respect to the end of bearing the distinctively Christian witness of faith and, therefore, so far as theology is concerned, an authority for determining the appropriateness of its assertions.

The result of considering the first issue, then, is to sharpen our original question. Granted that it is solely with respect to determining the appropriateness of theological assertions that scripture can be an authority for theology at all, is there any sense in which, in this respect, it alone is the primary theological authority?

2. *The Nature of Theological Authority*

Essential to any answer to this question is further consideration of the nature of theological authority. And this requires, in turn, that we employ the conclusions, even if we do not develop the arguments, of a philosophy of authority in general. Given the limits of this study, this part of the argument can be no more than an outline of the points that need to be made. Also, I claim no originality for the understanding of theological authority that I shall suggest. Details aside, I shall simply follow the treatments of this issue and of the larger issue of authority as such that other writers have presented more adequately (cf. Benn; Thielicke).

The first point can be made by observing the general distinction between *de facto* and *de jure* authority. Authority may be said to exist *de facto* whenever one person recognizes another, or some agent or instrument of another, as having the right to command or to act as regards his or her own action or belief. Thus scripture may be said to have a *de facto* authority for theology whenever a theologian recognizes that the writings of the canonical authors are entitled to function as a standard or norm for determining the appropriateness of his or her assertions to the Christian witness of faith. But aside from the fact that, as thus understood, *de facto* authority presupposes *de jure* authority, in the sense of the right to command or to act as regards the action or belief of others, it is clear that the authority claimed for scripture by the Protestant scriptural principle is more than a merely *de facto* authority. The point of this principle is not simply that scripture in fact *is* authoritative for theology because theologians recognize it to be so but that it by right *ought to be* thus authoritative whether they recognize its authority or not.

Yet it is true of any *de jure* authority, such as scripture is claimed to be, that its right to command or to act as regards the action or belief of others presupposes some rule or rules conferring this right and so authorizing it as an authority. In other words, all *de jure* authority is by logical necessity "rule-conferred authority." This is particularly obvious in the special case where one delegates authority to someone else to command or to act on one's behalf or in one's stead. Here, clearly, what is "done by authority" is "done by commission, or license from him whose right it is" (so Thomas Hobbes, as quoted by Benn: 215). But even in cases where the authority is undelegated, there can be *de jure* authority at all only where there is a preexisting rule or rules that confer it as a right and so authorize it. In general, then, one can speak of someone or something being or having authority, as distinct from the sheer power to control the action or belief of others, only when the authority or possessor of authority ultimately stands on the same level as those over whom he, she, or it is or has authority vis-à-vis the rule or rules conferring it. Thus, for example, both the judge and the accused who is subject to the judge's authority stand under the same laws and rules of justice, which are as binding on the judge's verdict as they are on the actions of the accused. Or again, the teacher no less than the student is subject to the demands of their particular discipline, which confront both of them alike in its constitutive methods of inquiry and procedures of verification.

What is thus true of authority in general is also true of theological authority, at least as Protestant theology has traditionally understood it. In this understanding, both the magisterium of the church and its particular tradition of doctrine and discipline are authorized in their authority by scripture and, therefore, ultimately stand on the same level in relation to scripture as those over whom they have their authority. Moreover, not even scripture is understood to be an exception to this rule when it, in turn, is claimed to have unique theological authority; for according to the so-called material principle of the Reformers, it is Christ alone who authorizes scripture as *norma normans, sed non normata.* Just because scripture is uniquely normative over all other theological sources or norms it itself ultimately stands on the same level as those who are subject to its authority vis-à-vis Jesus Christ.

Contrary, then, to a widely prevalent misunderstanding, it is no part of the authority claimed for scripture or for any other theological authority to deprive those who are subject to it of their own rights and responsibilities. This is so far from true, in fact, that the right of any theological authority, including scripture, to control the action or belief of every person under it necessarily implies his or her right and responsibility, in turn, to control it—namely, in relation to the rule or rules that alone authorize it, insofar as it is or has any authority at all. In this sense, any theological authority is by its very nature not only an authority that *is* authorized, but also an authority that *is to be* authorized by controlling its commands or actions in relation to the still higher authority, or source of authority, under which it stands. In traditional terms, any theological norm is not only *norma normata* but also *norma normanda*. It is the former insofar as it has already proved itself to those who stand under it and have thus controlled its right to control them; and it is the latter insofar as this right does not exclude but presupposes their continuing right and responsibility to control it.

But if every theological norm is itself "normed" and "to be normed" in this way, what of the claim traditionally made for scripture that it is the "norm that norms but is not normed"? The answer, I submit, is that this claim has traditionally served to distinguish scripture from all other recognized theological norms, not to deny that it itself is normed and is to be normed in relation to Jesus Christ. Given the material principle of the Reformers, scripture is and must be like any other theological authority in being or having an authorized authority. In this sense, it, too, is and must be a norm that is normed. But since what norms scripture is Christ himself, there is also an important sense in which it is not normed—namely, not by any other theological norm, properly so-called. Scripture is unlike all other theological authorities in that what authorizes it is not itself a theological authority in the proper sense of the words.

This implies, of course, that Christ, or the God whom he decisively re-presents, neither is nor has a theological authority—at any rate, in the same literal sense of the words, as distinct from such analogical sense as they may be given in distinguishing the persons of the trinity by speaking of the authority of the Son that is given him by the Father, and so forth. But this implication is to be accepted and insisted on for the reasons well expressed by Martin Luther: "Christ gives peace, not as the apostles gave it by preaching the gospel, but as its author and creator. The Father creates and gives life, grace, peace, and so on; the Son creates and gives the very same things" (40/1: 81). Although Christ, or God, is indeed the primal *source* of all authority, it is misled and misleading to say in any literal sense that (as one recent writer puts it) "Christianity recognizes only one absolute authority—that of God himself."

Such, in bare outline, is the understanding of theological authority that I take to be essential to our inquiry. If it can be accepted, the condition that must be fulfilled if one is to give a positive answer to our sharpened question should now be clear. Scripture can be in some sense the sole primary authority for determining the appropriateness of theological assertions if, but only if, it is the norm that norms but is not normed in the sense of this traditional claim that has now been clarified. But to ask whether this condition is fulfilled is to raise, in effect, the next basic issue that we must briefly consider—namely, whether the traditional claim is sound that scripture is the only canon of the Christian church, or whether the locus of this canon is in some still higher theological authority, as yet unrecognized, by which scripture itself is and is to be authorized.

3. The Locus of the Canon

According to Hans von Campenhausen, the concept of what is canonical "must be appropriate to the actual history of the canon" (1968: 2–3). Consequently, "it is arbitrary if, depending on one's taste, one makes liturgical use, or formal definition, or the idea of inspiration, or even official ecclesial confirmation the only criterion of what is canonical. Fundamental—corresponding to the meaning of the word—is the notion of the authoritativeness or normativeness that some writing or collection of writings has acquired for faith and life" (3). So far as the New Testament writings are concerned, "one can first speak of a 'canon' only where such a writing or group of writings is intentionally recognized to have a distinctive normative status, by virtue of which it stands alongside of the already existing Old Testament 'scripture'" (123).

Having established this, however, Campenhausen acknowledges that "the essential substance of what was eventually to form the New Testament is, naturally, earlier. This is the historical witness to Jesus Christ and to what he signifies—his salvation, his truth, and his word. From the beginning, this witness possesses a special sacredness and a special life-determining authority" (124). At first, the tradition of this witness "is exclusively oral, but, being of the highest spiritual significance, it is in no way arbitrary, but, rather, strives to attain permanent validity and hence tends toward a more or less fixed and permanent form. If the tradition acquires such definite, determinate form and is finally standardized and made binding in this form, one could speak of it as actually 'canonical'; for in this case it would already be the stage immediately prior to the later gospels and the New Testament in general, and writing it down would then add scarcely anything new in principle" (124).

The relevance of Campenhausen's observations is to make clear that for the most recent historical scholarship, even as, in a way, for the older orthodoxy, it is not essential to the concept of "canon" that has been applied to scripture that it can properly refer only to what has acquired a written form (cf. Schmid: 42). Essential to the concept, rather, is only that a witness of faith that is to be properly referred to as "canon" must have already acquired a linguistic form, oral or written, sufficiently fixed that it can function as a norm or standard for Christian faith and life, and thus also for determining the appropriateness of Christian theology. One could say in the Aristotelian terms of orthodoxy that, while a relatively fixed linguistic form belongs to the essence of the canon, the fact that its form also happens to be written is merely accidental. For the rest, the meaning of the term "canon" should already be clear enough. It is simply a synonym for "norm," in the unique sense of *norma normans, sed non normata* that was clarified above.

This implies, among other things, that "canon" must in the nature of the case be a systematically ambiguous term. On the Protestant understanding of theological authority previously outlined, the traditional reference of this term to scripture varies in meaning systematically according to the context in which it is being used. In one sense, it refers to the collection of writings produced by the early church and gradually recognized by it as being or having the sole primary authority for its faith, witness, and theology. In this sense, the canon undoubtedly expresses a decision, or more exactly, a whole history of decisions, on the part of the church. It is the product, indeed, of the *experientia ecclesiae*, at least in the sense that it emerged only in the course of the church's continuing attempts to control all putative authorities in relation to the primal source of all authority in Christ himself. But since "popes and councils can err," the canon that thus emerged from the early church's experience and decisions is and must be open to revision. As itself *norma normata* in relation to Christ, if not in relation to any other proper norm, the norm constituted by this collection of writings is also *norma normanda* in that whether, or to what extent, its authority is not only recognized by the church but also authorized by Christ remains and must remain an open question.

And just this is the other sense of "canon" that has to be taken into account—namely, not the collection of writings recognized as authoritative by the early church, but whatever of or in those writings is in fact authorized by Christ through the church's continuing experience under the guidance of the Holy Spirit. As Luther puts it decisively: "All the genuine sacred books agree in this, that they all preach and push Christ. And this is the true test by which to judge all books, when one sees whether they push Christ or not, since all scripture shows us Christ (Rom. 3), and Paul will know nothing but Christ (1 Cor. 2). What does not teach Christ is not apostolic, even though Peter or Paul teach it; again, what preaches Christ is apostolic even though Judas, Annas, Pilate, and Herod do it" (Luther: DB: 7: 384). How far Luther was prepared to carry this rejection of merely formal authority becomes clear from a passage such as the following: "Divine faith clings to the word that is God himself, believes, trusts, and honors this word—not for the sake of him who speaks it, but rather feels that it is so true and certain that no one can any longer tear it away. . . . The word itself, without any respect for persons, must do enough for the heart, must so grasp and convince one, that, caught up by it, one feels how true and right it would be even if the whole world . . . yes, even if God himself said otherwise" (as quoted by Bultmann, 1954: 108).

The early church itself in effect acknowledged the ambiguity of "canon" in that it subjected its decisions concerning the contents and limits of the New Testament to the criterion of apostolicity. Thus, according to Campenhausen, "one can well call the New Testament—considered as a 'canonical' collection—a creation of the post-Marcionite church. But on the other hand, the content of this New Testament collection of writings and, to some extent, even the writings themselves were already given to the church as 'apostolic witness.' The church knew itself to have been called into life by this witness and had not itself created the writings. It could merely accept, affirm, and confirm them. Thus one can also say with equal or even greater justification that the canon—conceived with respect to its content—imposed itself and was in any case not a work of the church on which it was binding" (1968: 381–382, n. 12).

Contrary to the opinion sometimes expressed, the church was by no means satisfied in reaching its decisions by merely formal claims to apostolic authorship. As Campenhausen rightly insists, "the apostolic title is not the presupposition but the result of a testing that took place in the first instance, not according to formal, but according to material, perspectives, historical as well as theological—for good or for ill, with the means that the science of the time had to offer" (1970: 121). Furthermore, the question of the apostolicity of writings was far from being a merely historical question of authorship as we today would understand such a question. Fundamental as its concern with authorship certainly was, there is every reason to suppose that the early church depended in part on theological considerations in determining it. "In general," according to Willi Marxsen, "one drew on criteria with respect to *content* in order to reach 'historical' judgments as to authorship. To this extent, one reasoned in a circle: only that could and should be canonical which was apostolic; if its apostolicity was uncertain, or was disputed, one considered its content. One asked whether its content agreed with what one took to be canonical—for one naturally supposed that one had the right doctrine in that one stood in the right apostolic tradition" (Marxsen, 1968a: 30).

Dubious as such reasoning surely is from the standpoint of modern historical criticism, it removes any doubt about the essential character of the early church's decisions concerning the New Testament canon. Just as the church recognized the Old Testament writings to be authoritative for itself only because it understood them to be the witness to Christ borne by the prophets, so it recognized the New Testament writings to be canonical only because it took them to be the witness to Christ borne by the apostles. In this way, the church's decisions were themselves controlled by the principle of apostolicity and, therefore, by the primal source of all authority in God's once-for-all revelation in

Jesus Christ. The unique authority it recognized in the apostles was understood to be due entirely to their being the direct witnesses of this revelation. Thus by asking whether a writing was apostolic, the early church asked, in effect, whether it "pushed Christ" in the unique sense of being authored by someone directly authorized by Christ himself.

To recognize this, however, is to understand, as Marxsen says, that "the 'canon' of the New Testament canon is apostolic authorship," in the sense that "this 'canon' provides the criterion for testing the canon of scripture" (33). By itself, of course, this understanding in no way entitles one to infer that the locus of the canon is anywhere else than in the writings of the New Testament and, for analogous reasons, in those of the Old Testament as well—as is signalled by the fact that Marxsen himself sets the word "canon" in quotation marks in speaking thus of "the 'canon' of the New Testament canon." But such an inference *is* warranted—indeed, mandatory—insofar as the early church's claims for the apostolic authorship of the New Testament writings are no longer tenable, and insofar as there is some other witness of faith whose linguistic form is sufficiently fixed that it can be properly referred to as "canon." Just these, however, are two conclusions strongly supported by the generally accepted results of modern historical-critical study of the New Testament.

It is now commonly acknowledged that none of the New Testament writings in its present form was authored by an apostle or by one of his disciples. Even the authentic letters of Paul come from one who was only indirectly in apostle in this sense, in that he was not a witness of Jesus' earthly life, having seen only the risen Lord. On the other hand, literary analysis of the New Testament, and especially form criticism of the synoptic gospels, has succeeded within limits in identifying the original witness of the apostolic church, of which all the canonical writings are, at one stage or another, later interpretations. The inference is unavoidable, then, precisely insofar as one insists on applying the early church's own criterion of apostolicity, that the locus of the *auctoritas canonica* is not the New Testament itself, to say nothing of the Old, but the original witness that is prior to the New Testament, although accessible to us today only by way of historical reconstruction from it. In Marxsen's words, "the norm for the church, therefore, is not the New Testament but, rather, the *apostolic witness*. This witness is, of course, found in the New Testament, but it is not identical with the New Testament" (34). "In the strict sense only the apostolic testimony to Jesus as the Divine revelation can be described as canonical. On the other hand, however, this Canon can only be arrived at via the New Testament. . . . the enquiry concerning Jesus always leads us back through one of the lines of proclamation present in the New Testament to the Canon which is prior to the New Testament" (1968b: 283). Elsewhere Marxsen elaborates this conclusion as follows:

We can accept the (thoroughly correct) dogmatic concern of the early church to establish the *auctoritas canonica* with the help of the 'apostolic principle.' If we then arrive at a different result, finding the *auctoritas canonica* in another place, this depends on the contingency of our existence in our own time, which binds us to our own methods. We maintain the concern of the early church precisely when we control its result. At stake is, indeed, the 'closed canon.' But this by no means has to be present in the form of a canon of writings. It is in principle indifferent whether the apostolic witness is present, or is to be reconstructed, in written form, or whether it is formulated only orally and has come to us through tradition in this oral formulation (which theorectically, at least, is entirely conceivable). The demand for a closed canon, which we can agree with in principle, may not be precipitately equated with the demand for a closed canon of writings, with an eye on the one already existing. At stake is not at all a new determination of the limits of the canon, but a new more exact determination of the *locus* of the canon. . . . In my opinion, one can no longer speak of the *auctoritas canonica* of the canon of scripture. This *auctoritas* belongs, rather, exclusively to the apostolic witness (1969: 135).

4. *The Validity of the Scriptural Principle*

If this conclusion is to the point, we today must indeed recognize a higher theological authority than the canon of scripture, and hence can no longer maintain that scripture is the sole primary authority for Christian theology. The theological authority of scripture, great as it may be, is nevertheless a limited authority, in that it could conceivably be greater than it is—namely, as great as that of the apostolic witness by which it itself is and is to be authorized. Indeed, relative to Christ himself and to the apostolic witness that alone is directly authorized by him, there is no difference in principle but only in fact between the authority of scripture, on the one hand, and that of the church's tradition and magisterium, on the other. Not only is the canon of scripture itself the product of the church's experience and decisions, but all the individual writings of the New Testament as well are expressions of the church's ongoing interpretation of the original apostolic witness. Therefore, we have every reason to accept the further conclusion that Marxsen draws with characteristic candor:

> . . . the alternative stated again and again from the Protestant side ever since the Reformation is no genuine alternative at all. According to the traditional formulation, we Protestants maintain 'sola scriptura' (canonical scripture alone), while the Catholics hold to 'scripture and tradition.' But this is not a real alternative; for whoever admits 'sola scriptura' (scripture alone), which is to say, the New Testament canon of Athanasius and the Synod of Rome, thereby also always admits tradition, the decision of the church. . . . Given the alternative, 'scripture alone' or 'scripture and tradition,' the Roman Catholic Church undoubtedly has the better position; for (this I say quite bluntly) whoever admits sola scriptura, in the sense of holding that the canonical New Testament is the sole norm, rule, and standard, goes the way of the Roman Catholic—only not as consistently (1968a: 26).

And yet important as it is that these conclusions be accepted, the basic issue of the validity of the scriptural principle remains to be considered. Aside from the fact that, on any account, scripture occupies a unique place with respect to the theological task, a hasty abandonment of sola scriptura as simply invalid jeopardizes more fundamental theological motives to which no Protestant, at least, can be indifferent, and it may very well also be seriously confusing as to the remaining theological alternatives. Accordingly, without in any way withdrawing the conclusions already reached, I wish to make three comments on the basic issue by way of delimiting them.

The first comment is that, from the standpoint of the Reformers, certainly, the formal principle sola scriptura neither is nor can be an independent theological principle. On the contrary, it must always be understood in relation to the material principle solus Christus which implies, in turn, the further material principles sola gratia and sola fide. As we have seen, Luther leaves no doubt that the unique theological authority of scripture is derived solely from the event of Christ to which it is the original witness, and this means, naturally, the event in which God decisively justifies human beings by grace alone through faith alone without the works of the law. Christ is properly preached, Luther insists, only "when that Christian freedom that he bestows is rightly taught" (Luther: 7: 59). It is just because or insofar as scripture originally preaches Christ in this way that it is apostolic and truly scriptural, and hence is the sole primary authority for theology as well as for faith and witness. Consequently, even if our historical understanding of scripture today makes *sola scriptura* untenable, one need not suppose, and I should think ought not suppose, that it does not in its own way—out of the contingency of another time and other methods—express valid, indeed, crucial theological motives.

This leads to the second comment that the alternatives to the traditional scriptural principle are not exhausted either by the Catholic principle "scripture and tradition" or by the spiritualistic appeal to the *Christus praesens*, or the internal witness of the Holy Spirit, divorced from any external canonical authority (Ritschl). There remains the distinct alternative—and, in my judgment, the only correct alternative—of following the intention of the scriptural principle itself and relocating the *auctoritas externa* in the original witness that both constituted the apostolic church and, in another sense, was constituted by it. Just as the early church's criterion of apostolicity, when applied under the conditions of our present historical methods and knowledge, points to this original witness as alone canonical in the strict sense, so adherence to the motives expressed by the Reformers' principle *sola scriptura* leads, under the same conditions, to precisely this apostolic witness as the true *norma normans, sed non normata*.

Of course, it must be said of this witness, even as the Reformers said of scripture, that it is Christ alone who is the source of its authority, so that it, too, is normed, even if not by any other norm properly so-called. But, then, it must also be said, conversely, that the Christ who is Lord of the apostolic witness, even as he is, in Luther's words, "King of scripture" (*rex scripturae*), is none other than the Jesus whom this witness attests to be the Christ (40/1: 459). This is just the point of Luther's characterization of scripture as "queen": "This queen ought to rule, and all ought to obey and be subject to her. They ought not to be masters, judges, or arbiters, but only witnesses, disciples, and confessors—whether it be the Pope, Luther, Augustine, Paul, or an angel from heaven. Nor ought any other doctrine be taught and heard in the church except the pure word of God" (120).

Marxsen underscores this point in replying to the objection that it is unwarranted to presuppose that the normative witness to Christ has to be found in the earlier New Testament writings. Although he grants that the later Gospel of John can indeed be closer to the witness to Christ than the earlier synoptic gospels, this is because all later interpretations have to be controlled with respect to their material, not merely their temporal, proximity to the original witness. But in the case of this original witness itself, he insists, "the material and the temporal perspectives coincide." Therefore, while one cannot ask simply for the *earlier writings*, everything does depend on asking for the *"earliest traditions"* (1969: 134–135, n. 9). Marxsen's point, I take it, is not to hold (as his talk of a coincidence of material and temporal perspectives might appear to imply) that the earliest traditions accessible to us are beyond the possibility, or exempt from the necessity, of critical interpretation in relation to that which alone endows them with their unique authority. He wishes to stress, rather, that in this unique case, the distinction that necessarily remains between any theological authority and that which authorizes it is no longer also a *temporal* distinction between a later witness and an earlier one, but is the strictly *hermeneutical* distinction between what is said and what is meant in these earliest traditions of witness themselves. Thus even though it is solely the Christ meant in these traditions who authorizes what they say, it is solely through what they say that we have directly to do with the Christ who is the source of their and, through them, all other theological authority. To this extent, the New Testament designations of the apostles as well as Christ himself as the "foundation" of Christian existence (cf. Eph. 2:20 and Rev. 21:14 with 1 Cor. 3:11) are theologically justified. By its very nature, Christian faith is apostolic faith—faith *with* the apostles in the Jesus to whom they uniquely are the witnesses and who is himself personally present as the Christ in *their* witness of faith.

This implies, naturally, rejection of the familiar claim that it is "the so-called historical Jesus" who is the sole primary authority for theology. Against any such claim, Martin Kähler's argument still has force that the final theological appeal, rather, is and must be to "the historic, biblical Christ," although, given the necessary relocation of the canon in the earliest witness of the church, this phrase needs to be replaced by "the historic, *apostolic* Christ," understood to mean "the Jesus attested by the apostolic witness" (Kähler). As for Kähler's concern in arguing against liberal life-of-Jesus theology that the faith and witness of the church not be made dependent on a papacy of the historians, two points should be kept in mind.

First of all, to be a source of faith and witness is one thing; to be the sole primary authority for theology, something else. Therefore, even if it is not the New Testament itself but the apostolic witness that preceded it which is the primary authority for the appropriateness of theological assertions, this in no way entails that the canon of scripture cannot be a source—even in a sense the only primary source—of the one witness of faith to which all Christian faith and witness from the apostles on are the response. Marxsen likes to say that "the New Testament is the oldest extant volume of the church's preaching" (1968a: 51). But if this is true, as, in principle, it certainly is, there clearly is a sense in which it is the New Testament itself, not the apostolic witness that must be historically reconstructed from it, that is and remains the sole primary source of Christian faith and witness. Then, second, the fact that the primary theological authority is not the historical Jesus but the apostolic witness by no means implies that the primal source of all authority could be anything other than Jesus himself or that theology could have to do with this source otherwise than through historical-critical inquiry. "The historic, apostolic Christ," just like "the historic, biblical Christ," is every bit as historical as "the so-called historical Jesus," and to this extent there is no escaping the dependence of theology on the work of the historians. On the contrary, we must insist that historical-critical inquiry is *theologically* necessary and legitimate (Strecker: 476).

The third and last comment is that, even with the relocation of the canon in the apostolic witness, scripture retains a unique place over against the rest of the church's tradition and magis-

terium with respect to determining the appropriateness of theological assertions. Even as the Christ who is the only primal
source of theological authority is the Christ with whom we directly have to do solely through the apostolic witness to Jesus,
so this witness itself is accessible to us only by way of historical
reconstruction from the writings of the New Testament. As
Marxsen puts it in a sentence already quoted, it is from these
writings that "we must always start, for the enquiry concerning
Jesus always leads us back through one of the lines of proclamation present in the New Testament to the Canon which is
prior to the New Testament." In short, scripture is, in a sense,
the only primary source not only of faith and witness but also
of theology. Although it is not itself the primary authority for
determining the appropriateness of theology's assertions, it is
the sole primary source in which this authority is to be found.

5. The Use of Scripture as a Theological Authority

There remains, finally, the issue of the actual use of scripture
as a theological authority. Of course, this issue has already been
settled in principle with the conclusions reached by the preceding argument. Because not even the New Testament is the canon
of the church, which is rather the apostolic witness to Jesus
Christ that is historically prior to the New Testament, the authority of scripture for determining the appropriateness of theological assertions is but a derived or secondary authority.
Consequently, merely to establish that an assertion is derived
from scripture or warranted by it is not sufficient to authorize
the assertion as theologically appropriate. It is further necessary
to establish that the scriptural source or warrant for the assertion
is itself authorized by the original witness of the apostles, which
is the sole primary authority for determining the appropriateness
of theological assertions.

But just what this means and does not mean in fact, or for
the actual use of scripture in theological reflection and argument,
needs to be further clarified. Such clarification is called for, in
the first place, because the procedures thus indicated in principle
may seem sufficiently similar to those of another, by now familiar, way of doing Protestant theology to be mistakenly identified with them. Then, in the second place, it can hardly be
clear from the little that has been said how, if at all, the Old

Testament, as well as the New, is to be used as an authority for determining the appropriateness of theological assertions. Accordingly, at least these two points must be cleared up if this study is to sketch even the outlines of a possible position on the authority of scripture for theology.

As for the first point, it is pertinent to recall that the same Luther who did not hesitate to criticize even the canonical writings by reference to Christ as the sole source of their authority could also speak out emphatically for the inspiration of scripture (cf. Pieper: 1: 334–335). In Protestant orthodoxy, then, the developed doctrine of the verbal inspiration of the canonical writings entailed the assertion of their uniform authority and thus made it possible to claim without qualification that "what Scripture says, God says" (Packer: 47). But with the emergence of Protestant liberal theology and its commitment to the historical-critical method, as well as its insistence that scripture neither is nor can be sufficient authorization for the truth of theological assertions, this claim was abandoned, never again to be made by those who have led in the subsequent developments in Protestant theology. Even the postliberal theologians whom we commonly speak of today as neo-orthodox typically distinguished between the Bible itself and the so-called biblical message contained in it, which alone is sufficient to authorize the assertions of Christian theology. Thus the general idea that the authority of the canon of scripture is, in a sense, secondary—namely, to "the canon within the canon" of the scriptural message—is not a new theological idea. As a matter of fact, it is only in the qualified sense allowed for by this idea, more consistently understood than it was by Luther, that the leading Protestant theologians of the twentieth century have been willing to maintain that scripture is the sole primary authority for theological assertions.

The thing to notice about this typically postliberal Protestant position, however, is that scripture, or, at any rate, the New Testament, is still in a sense, even if a highly qualified sense, the sole primary authority for Christian theology. Although, on this position, the authority of the New Testament derives entirely from the message that its various writings more or less adequately express, what this message is is to be determined by the critical interpretation of just these New Testament writings, and of them alone. In other words, "the canon within the canon" typically employed by neo-orthodoxy is the meaning to be discerned by critical interpretation of what is said in the canon of the New Testament as traditionally defined and acknowledged by the church. Thus while on this position, also, merely to establish that a theological assertion is derived from or warranted by something asserted in the New Testament is, indeed, insufficient to authorize it as appropriate, all that is further needed to authorize it is to establish its appropriateness to the New Testament message, which is itself determined by critical interpretation of the traditional canon.

But once this is noticed it should be clear why there is a fundamental difference between this familiar way of using scripture in theology and the procedures indicated here. The whole point of the preceding argument has been to show that it is no longer possible thus to presuppose the authority of the traditional canon. Given our present historical methods and knowledge, the locus of the canon—in the early church's own sense of the apostolic witness—cannot be the writings of the New Testament as such but can only be the earliest traditions of Christian witness accessible to us today by historical-critical analysis of these writings. Specifically, the canon of the church, and hence also the primary authority for theology, must now be located in what form critics generally speak of as the earliest layer of the synoptic tradition, or what Marxsen in particular refers to as "the Jesus-kerygma," as distinct both from "the Christ-kerygma" and from "the mixed form of the Jesus-kerygma and the Christ-kerygma" that we find expressed in the writings of the New Testament (1968a: 108–109, 111). Accordingly, the witness to which theological assertions must be appropriate is not the *scriptural* witness typically spoken of in most postliberal Protestant theology but, rather, the *apostolic* witness, which is to be discerned by critical interpretation of this earliest layer of Christian tradition or kerygma. But this means that the first essential procedure involved in the actual use of scripture as a theological authority is not so much hermeneutical as historical. Specifically, it is the historical procedure of reconstructing the history of tradition of which the writings of the New Testament are the documentation, so as thereby to identify the earliest layer in this tradition, from which alone the *true* "canon within the canon" is to be discerned.

To recognize the necessity for such reconstruction and identification, however, is to appreciate the real, indeed crucial, theological importance of the so-called new quest of the historical Jesus. Whether the methods of the new quest can achieve very much in the way of reliable historical knowledge about Jesus may well be doubted (cf. Strecker; Gager). Nevertheless, if the new quest is understood, as its methods require that it should be, as the identification and interpretation of the Jesus-kerygma of the earliest church, it may be said to perform the first essential task in the actual use of scripture as a theological authority. For "the canon within the canon" to which all theological assertions must be appropriate is the meaning to be discerned in the earliest layer of Christian witness, and this means the Jesus-kerygma of the apostolic community. It is in this kerygma that the Jesus who is the subject-term of all Christian witness, and hence the source of all theological authority, is attested without explicit christological predicates—the Christ-kerygma as such, as Marxsen has shown, being implicit in the "that" of the apostolic kerygma, as distinct from its "what" (Marxsen, 1960). Therefore, since all explicit christological predicates not only serve to interpret their subject-term but, more importantly, are also to be interpreted by it, it is the meaning to be discerned precisely in the Jesus-kerygma by which the appropriateness of all explicit christology and, consequently, all other theological assertions is to be judged.

This brings us to further clarification of the second point, concerning the use of the Old Testament, also, as a theological authority. The usual view on this point in recent Protestant theology is, in effect, this: just as the New Testament is to be used by theology only under the control of the New Testament message, so the Old Testament's authority for theological reflection and argument is subject to that of the New. But for the reasons I have just explained, this familiar view of the use of the Old Testament is now scarcely less untenable than the views of the Reformers and of the orthodox dogmaticians of which it is a revision. Because, given our present historical methods and knowledge, the true canon of the church must be located prior to the canon of scripture in the Jesus-kerygma of the earliest community, it is solely under the authority of this kerygma, and hence, ultimately, under the control of the meaning to be discerned in it, that the Old Testament, like the New, may be used as a theological authority.

But what can it mean to say even this about the use of the Old Testament? That the New Testament is to be used in theology only under the authority of the Jesus-kerygma poses no particular difficulty, since the New Testament writings, like the rest of the church's tradition and magisterium, expressly have to do with the subject-term of this kerygma, that is, with Jesus, even if in the different form of making more or less fully explicit in successive situations of the church's existence the christological claim that is merely implicit in the Jesus-kerygma as such. However, we now recognize that it is historically false as well as theologically misleading to claim that the Old Testament writings, too, are expressly about the Jesus who is the subject-term of all Christian witness and theology, beginning with the Jesus-kerygma of the earliest church. Recognizing this, or, in other words, recognizing that the Old Testament does not bear witness to Christ prophetically in the sense in which the early church understood it to do and, therefore, at the crucial point is *not* like the New, forces the question whether the Old Testament may be properly used as a theological authority at all. Of course, this is not a new question for Christian theology, having been raised in effect as soon as scripture came to be viewed as a collection of writings, the only adequate methods for dealing with which are the same historical-critical methods that must be employed in analyzing and interpreting any historical document. Still, if the Old Testament is to be used as a theological authority, even in the highly qualified way allowed for here, there is the question of how this can be done, given the methods and knowledge that must be accepted by theology today.

The key to an answer, I submit, is the insight that the writings of the Old Testament contain the most fundamental presuppositions, and thus provide all the main concepts, of the Jesus-kerygma of the earliest church. Put differently, the Old Testament writings document the particular linguistic form of the question of human existence—more exactly, of the ultimate meaning of human existence—to which the Jesus-kerygma presents itself as the answer (Bultmann, 1948–1953). True, the conceptual form of the Jesus-kerygma is shaped most immediately by that of late Jewish apocalypticism, which is now widely regarded as having provided the main concepts of early Christian witness and theology, as well as, presumably, of the witness of Jesus himself. But, without doubt, the necessary presuppositions of apocalypticism, and so also those of the Jesus-kerygma, are the express subject of the distinctive religious tradition whose foundations are documented by the Old Testament (Bultmann, 1949). Consequently, if theology asks, as it must, for the meaning of the Jesus-kerygma, and thus for the understanding of human existence—of ourselves, the world, and God—that the Jesus-kerygma necessarily presupposes, the answer, clearly, is that it is a certain form or development of the understanding of existence that is variously expressed in the writings of the Old Testament.

Logically speaking, then, one may say that the relation of the Old Testament to the earliest Christian witness is like that of the necessary presuppositions of an assertion to the assertion itself, or, alternatively, like that of a question to its answer. But if this is correct, there is no doubt that the Old Testament, in its way, is also a theological authority, nor does using it as such pose any particular difficulty. For in the nature of the case, the necessary presuppositions of an assertion must be as authoritative as the assertion itself, just as the authoritative answer to a question must endow the question itself with an equivalent authority.

This is not the place to pursue further the understanding of the Old Testament's authority thus briefly indicated, although I would express my conviction that it is not as different as it may seem from the early church's understanding that the Old Testament writings are authoritative for theology just because, or insofar as, they bear prophetic witness to Jesus Christ (cf. Bultmann, 1954: 313–336; 1952: 162–186). The relation of prophecy to fulfillment, even when properly interpreted, is not the same as that of presuppositions to assertion, or that of question to answer. And yet there is a considerable and important overlap between the two kinds of relation, which is all the more striking when we consider, as we must, that, in the case of the existential question, there logically cannot be any sharp distinction between question and answer and that the same is true as between the necessary presuppositions of a religious assertion and the assertion itself. But be this as it may, I trust it is now reasonably clear how the Old Testament as well as the New is to be used as a theological authority. Even though the Old Testament writings, unlike those of the New, do not expressly have Jesus as their subject, they do document the particular form of the existential question to which the Jesus-kerygma is the answer and, to this extent, are authoritative for determining the appropriateness of theological assertions.

Because this is so, however, there is evidently a further reason for the claim made earlier that, even on the position outlined in this study, the canon of scripture retains a unique place with respect to the theological task. For if the New Testament is the sole primary source in which the primary authority of Christian theology is to be found, the Old Testament is the sole primary source of the necessary presuppositions of this authority.

4

The Task of Philosophical Theology

This study consists in four theses, together with a minimum of development or elaboration of each of their main points. Since the issue they are designed to explore is precisely the task of philosophical theology, the crucial thesis is the third, to which the first two are ordered simply as essential presuppositions. By this I mean that neither of these theses is developed as fully as, given other aims, it could and should be developed, and that, therefore, much of what is said in these parts of the study is particularly vulnerable to criticism. On the other hand, given my own interest in the issue of philosophical theology, which, I suspect, is not at all untypical, the fourth thesis and its elaboration occupy a much larger part of the whole than might otherwise be the case. But the fact of the matter is that my concern with this issue is entirely that of a Christian theologian struggling for greater clarity about his distinctive task and responsibility, and I see only gain in this being taken fully into account.

1. *To exist as a self at all is possible solely on the basis of faith, so that the statement, "Unless you believe, you shall not understand," is true in a sense not only of the Christian or of the religious believer but of every human being simply as such.*

The import of this first thesis could be made fully clear only by a complete philosophical theology, which would consist for the most part simply in developing its manifold implications and presuppositions. Therefore, the important point now is not to anticipate such development, but to recognize the irreversible priority of faith in human existence. To exist in the characteristically human way is to exist by faith, for what is meant by "faith" is fundamentally that elevation of animal feeling and vitality to self-consciousness which constitutes the distinctively human mode of being.

In this connection, we may recall that an animal lacking in such self-consciousness nevertheless lives by what George Santayana calls "animal faith," meaning thereby the animal's instinctive confidence in its environment as permissive of its struggles to live and to reproduce its kind. According to Santayana, such faith is "the initial expression of animal vitality in the sphere of mind, the first announcement that anything is going on. It is involved in any pang of hunger, of fear, or of love. It launches the adventure of knowledge" (Santayana: 180–181). To speak so is, to be sure, to run the risks of anthropomorphism, and a phrase like "*instinctive* confidence" (or "*animal* faith") may, in view of what has just been said about the meaning of "faith," be plausibly regarded as a category mistake. But this should not obscure the fact that there is a significant continuity between the animal and the human levels of behavior. To live in either case is one and the same with accepting the larger setting of one's life and adjusting oneself to it. The difference in the human case is that the acceptance and adjustment in question are not merely instinctive but are more or less self-conscious acts. Thus it has been well said that a human being not only lives his or her life but also leads it (Gehlen; Plessner).

Yet if this is so, if to live one's life humanly is to lead it self-consciously, and in this sense to live by faith, it is also true that a human being is in a unique sense a being who can understand. Actually, so to formulate the matter obscures an important overlapping or coincidence in the meanings of "faith" and "understanding." If, as has been stated, to exist by faith is fundamentally to accept one's life and its setting and to adjust oneself to them in a self-conscious way, then faith itself, as already involving self-consciousness, is a mode of understanding. Hence it is indifferent whether we say that one exists humanly solely on the basis of faith or say, rather, that one never exists humanly except as a being who understands. But this in no way retracts the irreversible priority of faith which is the point of the first thesis. The mode of understanding that faith itself is or involves, or, as we may say, the understanding of faith, *genitivus subjectivus*, is always to be distinguished from, because it is irreversibly prior to, the different mode of understanding whereby faith itself may be understood, or, in other words, the understanding of faith, *genitivus objectivus*. The explanation of this difference is that one is more than merely animal not only in one's understanding relation to oneself and to the reality around oneself but in one's capacity to subject just such understanding to reflective analysis and interpretation of a higher order. In short, one not only understands but can understand that one understands—or, because "faith," too, is systematically ambiguous in the same general way, one not only believes but can believe that one believes.

There are alternative ways in which philosophers have given expression to this important difference—for instance, by distinguishing, as Alfred North Whitehead does, between the "practical reason" that Ulysses shares with the foxes and the "theoretical reason" that Plato shares with the gods (Whitehead, 1929: 10). But for our purposes here, it will be convenient to distinguish between the *existential* understanding or faith that is constitutive of human existence as such and the *reflective* understanding or faith whereby what is presented existentially can be re-presented in an express, thematic, and conceptually precise way. Given this distinction of levels, we may do justice not only to the insight that "unless you believe (existentially), you shall not understand (reflectively)," but also to the truth that existential faith itself belongs to the distinctively human level of life, and so is a mode of understanding rather than mere animal feeling and vitality.

Obviously, this distinction also enables us to clarify the important question of the relation between faith and reason. In the broad sense, "reason," like "understanding" or "self-consciousness," refers comprehensively to the distinctively human mode of being, and so coincides in meaning with "faith" likewise taken broadly. Insofar, however, as we follow the common usage whereby "reason" is understood more strictly as referring to *reflective* reason, while "faith" is taken to mean *existential* faith, reason and faith are quite properly said to be different and to be so related that faith always precedes reason, not the other way around. The importance of saying this is that one thereby clearly affirms the essentially derived and secondary function of reflective reasoning, whether as the logical analysis of ideas or as the translogical assessment of experiential evidence. The whole of human life, including our reflective life, is based on our existential faith, so that "reason" in the strict sense, or as referring to reflective reason in its several different forms, can be defined only as "faith seeking understanding," or, in R. G. Collingwood's variation on Anselm's phrase, "faith cultivating itself" (Rubinoff [ed.]: 108–121, 122–147). One implication of this is that there is a necessary limit to all attempts at rational justification. The existential faith by which we live neither needs justification nor can ever be justified. Rather, it is the very ground of justification, which pertains, therefore, to those re-presentations of itself in reflection which it belongs to human reason to provide (cf. Wittgenstein: 136).

One further precision that seems required is that "faith" as it is used here is not intended in a persuasive or eulogistic sense. For reasons both understandable and legitimate, "faith" is commonly taken to mean simply true or authentic faith, somewhat as "worth" is taken to mean only good, or "value," exclusively positive value. And yet the least reflection discloses that this natural restriction of meaning can be and often is misleading as to the full import of "faith" and its cognate terms. Even a false or inauthentic faith, which we sometimes speak of as "unfaith," is not simply the absence of faith but faith itself in its negative mode, rather as evil is the negative mode of worth, or disvalue is the negative mode of value. This explains why an animal lacking in self-consciousness, and thus incapable of believing in the distinctively human way, likewise could not be said to "disbelieve" in the sense in which the word is applicable to a human being. Accordingly, in affirming that we all unavoidably live by faith, I am in no way affirming or implying that the faith that constitutes our existence is necessarily authentic, and still less do I mean that our re-presentations of such faith through reflection must always be true. Rather, I am simply pointing to the fundamental condition of the possibility of distinguishing faith as (existentially) authentic or inauthentic and as (reflectively) true or false and am claiming that this condition is and must be our basic existential faith itself.

2. *Philosophy in general is the fully reflective understanding of the basic existential faith that is constitutive of human existence.*

"Philosophy," Whitehead says, "is an attitude of mind toward doctrines ignorantly entertained" (Whitehead, 1938: 233). But true as this is, it fails to specify wherein the undertaking that is properly philosophy differs from the generic "rationalism" that is the gift and the task of human reflection. The *differentia specifica* of philosophy is not in its being a reflective "attitude of mind" but in the particular kind of "doctrines" toward which this attitude is directed in the case of philosophical reflection. Such "doctrines," I maintain, are those comprised in our basic existential faith as selves, although, naturally, they may very well be "ignorantly entertained" in the sense that we do not yet hold them in mind with full self-consciousness of their meaning. Accordingly, insofar as philosophy may in any sense be called a "science," it can only be an absolutely basic and comprehensive science which seeks just such a reflective understanding of the faith that grounds and encompasses the whole of our life and thought.

Yet philosophy is like all reflection in being by its very nature historical. This means not only that it is always done by human beings faced with the limitations and opportunities of particular cultural situations, but also that it can scarcely hope to attain its object except through critico-constructive discussion with the tradition of understanding in which this object is already directly or indirectly reflected. To be sure, any such discussion would be impossible but for the preunderstanding that is always given in existential faith itself. But since the task of philosophy is to understand such existential faith at the level of full self-consciousness, in an express, thematic, and conceptually precise way, it can hardly afford to neglect the contributions to this task that are already expressed or implied in the whole tradition of human culture.

This is Whitehead's point in answering the question, "Where is the evidence?" "The answer is evidently human experience as shared by civilized intercommunication. The expression of such evidence, so far as it is widely shared, is to be found in law, in moral and sociological habits, in literature and art as ministering to human satisfactions, in historical judgments on the rise and decay of social systems, and in science. It is also diffused throughout the meanings of words and linguistic expressions. Philosophy is a secondary activity. It meditates on this variety of expression" (96–97; cf. 1933: 291–292). Elsewhere Whitehead adds that "the best rendering" of "that ultimate, integral experience . . . whose elucidation is the final aim of philosophy" is "often to be found in the utterances of religious aspiration" (1978: 208).

Whitehead's answer suggests two further points of some importance: first, that the "evidence" that philosophy must attend to comprises nothing less than the whole of human life and culture; and second, that the properly philosophical element in culture has relatively less evidential force than the other elements on which philosophy in the strict sense is always but the reflection. Whitehead himself makes this second point explicitly when he says that "philosophy must found itself upon the presuppositions and the interpretations of ordinary life. In our first approach to philosophy, learning should be banished. We should appeal to the simple-minded notions issuing from ordinary civilized social relations" (1938: 17; cf. 235–236). In fact, "the metaphysical rule of evidence" requires that "we must bow to those presumptions, which, in despite of criticism, we still employ for the regulation of our lives. Such presumptions are imperative in experience. Rationalism is the search for the coherence of such presumptions" (1978: 151).

It will be clear from what has been said that philosophy necessarily has both a critico-analytic and a constructive-synthetic aspect or function. Insofar as its aim is the reflective understanding of our basic existential faith, or, as Whitehead puts it, the "elucidation" of "that ultimate, integral experience, unwarped by the sophistications of theory," philosophy is unavoidably criticism and analysis, especially of language as expressive of human life and faith (208). And this, of course, is the justification for the widespread contemporary conviction that philosophy simply is the analysis of language. But since even those who share this conviction recognize that philosophy's concern is different from philology's, because it is with the "depth grammar" of our language, and hence with disclosing the "tacit presuppositions" of our forms of speaking and with mapping their "logical frontiers," the claim is pertinent that "the impulse behind that concern is *metaphysical*, not linguistic" (Passmore: 78). In any case, the historical function of philosophical analysis and criticism (and no great philosopher has ever failed to perform this function) has always been for the sake of philosophy's controlling function of synthesis and construction. Precisely in meditating on the "variety of expression" that makes up the history of human life and culture, philosophy always has aimed, and quite properly should aim, to lay bare the faith by which every one exists simply as a human being, together with the structure of reality as revealed to such faith.

Thus, for all its value, the conception of philosophy as solely or mainly analysis is abstract and one-sided and must give way to the more inclusive conception represented by Whitehead: "Philosophy is the attempt to make manifest the fundamental evidence as to the nature of things. Upon the presupposition of this evidence, all understanding rests. A correctly verbalized philosophy mobilizes this basic experience which all premises presuppose. It makes the content of the human mind manageable; it adds meaning to fragmentary details; it discloses disjunctions and conjunctions, consistencies and inconsistencies. Philosophy is the criticism of abstractions which govern special modes of thought," and its aim is "sheer disclosure." "If you like to phrase it so, philosophy is mystical. For mysticism is direct insight into depths as yet unspoken. But the purpose of philosophy is to rationalize mysticism: not by explaining it away, but by the introduction of novel verbal characterizations, rationally coordinated" (1938: 67, 237).

As it has developed historically, the one general task of philosophical understanding has been divided into any number of more special tasks. The reasons for this are not only the growing differentiation of human culture and the need for a division of labor even within philosophy, but also the inherently abstract character of human interest and reflection, which makes anything like a complete reflective understanding extremely difficult, if not impossible. A still more fundamental reason is that our existential faith itself is nothing utterly simple or lacking in complexity, but, at best, a unity-in-diversity or a structured whole involving several constitutive moments. In fact, one is tempted to say that we live not so much by faith as by faiths, by a number of basic beliefs whose exact relation to one another we may well discover to be an existential as well as a reflective problem.

Thus, for example, there is the basic belief tacitly presupposed by our whole enterprise of scientific explanation as organized in the various special sciences. This is the belief that the world of events of which we are part is so ordered that our experience of phenomena in the past and the present warrants our having certain expectations of the future. Or to give another example, there is the belief underlying all our moral behavior and language that some course of action open to us ought to be followed and that it ought to be a course which, so far as possible, includes the realization rather than the frustration of the various relevant interests affected by our action. These beliefs certainly are not the only ones that might be mentioned, and simply mentioning them is far from expressing an adequate understanding of their places in the faith by which we live. But it may at least make clear why special inquiries like the philosophy of science and the philosophy of morals (or, as it is usually called, moral philosophy or ethics) have been implicit in philosophical reflection right from the start and were bound to emerge as special disciplines, given a requisite differentiation of culture and specialization of labor. It may also suggest that a similar explanation is to be sought for such other inquiries as the philosophy of art, the philosophy of law, and the philosophy of religion—to mention only a few that might need to be considered.

Yet there is reason to hold that the philosophies of science, art, law, religion, etc., are all peripheral philosophical disciplines and are important, in the final analysis, only in relation to philosophy's central task of metaphysics. This is not the place to develop the concept of metaphysics so as to do justice both to its long and diverse history and to all it might be reconceived to mean, assuming the conception of philosophy in general as the fully reflective understanding of our common faith. But this much, at least, may be said.

Historically, metaphysics has been conceived from its beginnings as the noncompressible core of philosophy, understood as an absolutely basic and comprehensive science. As such, it eventually came to be differentiated into *metaphysica generalis*, or ontology, which is the understanding of the completely general features of reality, and *metaphysica specialis*, as comprising psychology, cosmology, and philosophical (or "natural") theology, which are devoted respectively to understanding the three basic realities of the self, the world, and God. Needless to say, this conception of the exact scope and content of metaphysics reflects the material metaphysical conclusions of the main tradition of Western philosophy. But even in the case of philosophies which reject these conclusions—which deny, say, that God is ultimately real, or else so radically reinterpret what "God" means that philosophical theology is in effect reduced to cosmology or psychology—the essential structure of metaphysical inquiry may still be readily discerned. It invariably involves the most basic and comprehensive questions that can occur to the human mind, and the procedure it follows in answering these questions always involves some form or other of the transcendental method, by which I mean simply the raising to full self-consciousness of the basic beliefs that are the necessary conditions of the possibility of our existing or understanding at all. In other words, metaphysics is the vital center of the entire critico-constructive undertaking that is philosophical reflection. It is for its sake, ultimately, that all the special philosophical inquiries exist, for they are really so many contributions to its one central task: to reflect on the faith by which we live and in this way to understand the nature of reality as disclosed to this faith.

To avoid misunderstanding, I would add that I have no intention here of presenting anything like an exhaustive analysis of "philosophy." Nothing at all has been said about such important philosophical disciplines as logic and epistemology, and there has been no attempt whatever at a systematic classification in which all the disciplines could be assigned their proper places. Since any such classification seems bound to be incomplete and more or less arbitrary, there is probably limited value in trying to work one out. Nevertheless, if the understanding of philosophy proposed here is at all correct, it should be possible on its basis to give a plausible account of all the forms of philosophical reflection and to classify them systematically in a way that is at least as valuable as any other. My hunch is that this can in fact be done, and in such a manner as to offer a convincing confirmation of the second thesis. But actually doing it must be left to another occasion.

3. *The task of philosophical theology, which is integral to philosophy's central task as metaphysics, is so to understand our common faith as to answer the basic question of the reality of God.*

It seems clear enough that the question of the reality of God first arises within the particular field of life and culture that is commonly distinguished as "religion." To be sure, we shall soon see that so basic a concept as "God," precisely as understood by religion (at least in certain of its forms), is bound to have a much broader basis than religion alone could possibly account for. But we shall hardly wish to question that it is as a religious concept that "God" is first made explicit and that its religious use is and remains its primary use. Even so, to those of us who stand within the predominantly theistic religious tradition of the West, it may still seem strange to say that it is within religion that the reality of God first becomes a *question*. Is it not the case, rather, that God's reality is the ultimate presupposition of religion, that "God" is its "constitutive concept," analogous, say, to the concept of "physical object" in science or of "obligation" in morality (Hudson: 61, 65)?

For *theistic* religion, this certainly is the case, as any philosophical analysis of its "form of life" will readily confirm. And yet the concept of "nontheistic religion" is not on the face of it self-contradictory and does in fact seem to be illustrated several times over among the phenomena studied by the historian of religions. Moreover, even among the religions that are in a broad sense "theistic," for which in one way or another "God" *is* a "constitutive concept," there is sufficient variety to require the familiar typologies distinguishing between polytheism, henotheism, and monotheism, pantheism, deism, and theism, etc. To this extent, the reality of God is already a question for religion itself, as the question both how the concept "God" is to be understood and whether on some understanding it refers to anything ultimately real. How much more, then, must it be a question for a properly conceived philosophy of religion, which refuses to restrict its evidence to anything less than the whole of our religious faith and life as a human community?

In reflecting on this evidence, however, the philosopher of religion can hardly fail to be struck by an essential difference between all that is specifically religious and the other fields of human life and culture. Unlike science, art, morality, and politics, religion cannot be adequately accounted for simply as one more form of life among several others. For all the obvious specificity of its beliefs, rites, and social organizations, it presents itself as having to do with the ultimate basis of our entire existence and therefore as fundamental to, not merely coordinate with, all the other cultural fields. In other words, religion in general is the primary and most direct reflection of the basic existential faith that constitutes human existence. Although its doctrines, for instance, have their origin in a quite particular occasion of insight or "special revelation," they are invariably put forward as having a general application and, in the case of the great world religions, as being universally valid. This is why Whitehead observes that "the doctrines of rational religion aim at being that metaphysics which can be derived from the supernormal experience of mankind in its moments of finest insight" (1926: 32).

But if the doctrines of developed religion aim at being metaphysics, the question of God's reality, which religion poses for philosophical understanding, is in its logic a metaphysical question. This is amply confirmed by the concept of "God" itself, particularly as it finally emerges from the immanent developments of religious history. Where God is conceived radically, as in monotheistic religions such as Judaism and Christianity, God is clearly understood as metaphysically real and so as not even possibly the object of strictly empirical modes of knowledge. As "the Father Almighty, Maker of heaven and earth, and of all things visible and invisible," God is understood to be the ultimate creative source of anything that is so much as possible, and hence to be in the strictest sense necessary, not merely a being among others, but in some way "being-itself." In fact, the God of theism in its most fully developed forms is the one metaphysical individual, the sole being whose individuality is constitutive of reality as such and who, therefore, is the inclusive object of all our faith and understanding.

This explains, of course, why philosophical theology has been traditionally understood as one of the subdisciplines of metaphysics. Because "God" is the metaphysical concept par excellence, the question of how this concept is to be understood and whether it refers to anything real can be answered only as a metaphysical question. The same reason, however, requires us to recognize a definite limitation in the traditional distinctions between *metaphysica generalis* and *metaphysica specialis* and between the three subdisciplines of which the second is held to be comprised. Although it may be useful for some purposes to distinguish ontology as the elucidation of strictly general features of reality, or "transcendentals," the fact remains that the distinction between the God of radical theism and all other things is itself a transcendental distinction, because God is conceived to be the one individual whose being and function are themselves strictly general. Consequently, if theism is true, God cannot be regarded as a third special object along with the self and the world, and ontology itself must be theology, even as theology must be ontology.

Furthermore, on a theistic view, neither the self nor the world is a metaphysical individual in the same sense that God is. To be sure, for a neoclassical theism such as I would defend, the world definitely is metaphysical, insofar as the reality of *some* world is no mere contingent fact but is a strictly general, and so necessary, feature of reality as such. But by "world," properly speaking, we refer not to *an* individual but to a *collection* of individuals, which is more than a mere collection without order or integrity, thanks only to the universal immanence of God as its sole primal source and final end. By "self," on the other hand, we do indeed refer to an individual that is unlike the world in being a concrete, integrated whole of reality, and to this extent an image or analogy of God. And yet the self is no more than God's image or analogy because its individuality, unlike God's, is not metaphysical in the sense of being ultimately constitutive of reality itself. True, the self is constitutive of our *understanding* of reality, insofar as it is in its basic existential faith alone that reality so presents itself that it can be understood, whether existentially or reflectively. To this extent, therefore, the self is an object of metaphysical reflection; and psychology (or, as we would no doubt say today, anthropology) is an integral metaphysical task along with theology and cosmology—as is evident from the fact that the self's denial of its own existence shares in the inescapable self-contradiction of all denials of metaphysical truth. Even so, the theistic view of the matter is that it belongs to the self's own essential self-affirmation to distinguish both itself and the world as but fragmentary parts of the one integral whole whose individuality alone suffices to constitute the very being of reality as such.

Thus Charles Hartshorne only states the obvious point of any radical theism when he says that "the import of the word 'God' is no mere special meaning in our language, but the soul of significance in general, for it refers to the Life in and for which all things live." And he draws the correct implication for the question of God which philosophical theology has to answer: "The theistic question . . . is not one more question, even the most important one. It is, on the fundamental level, and when all its implications are taken into account, the sole question. . . . Philosophy as a nonempirical study has no other subject matter" (1962: 297, 131–132).

Strictly speaking, of course, there could be no philosophical theology at all unless theism in some form (including, perhaps, pantheism and deism as well as theism proper) were metaphysically true. But this is simply to say that the alternative to a metaphysics that answers the question of God affirmatively (which, on my view, is all that "philosophical theology" can properly mean) is another metaphysics that answers it negatively—in short, an atheistic metaphysics. Since the question of God is by its very nature metaphysical, it cannot be answered one way or the other except metaphysically, by showing transcendentally that God either is or is not the inclusive object of all our faith and understanding, and hence is necessarily affirmed or necessarily denied by whatever we believe or understand. Because a positivistic philosophy that denies the meaningfulness of metaphysical assertions thereby answers this question, it is itself metaphysical, and atheistically so at that. For if metaphysics were impossible, God would be impossible, and this could be so only if the faith by which we exist, and so our metaphysics as well, were by their very nature atheistic. But it is just as true that no metaphysics can fail to answer the theistic question either affirmatively or negatively. As Hartshorne puts it, "Neutrality as to God means no metaphysics," for "if metaphysics knows anything, it must either know God, or know that the idea of God is meaningless" (1953: 176; cf. 1967: 32). Here it should be kept in mind that metaphysical understanding, like human reflection generally, moves between the two extremes of vagueness as to its meanings and recognition of their incoherence, with one another or with experience. Hence, while there may very well be a "metaphysics" that is neutral on the question of God, this is only because its meanings are so indefinite that it does not really know anything, and so is not really a metaphysics after all.

It follows from the strictly metaphysical character of the question of God that any argument for, or proof of, God's reality, as well as any counterargument or disproof, can only be metaphysical. Hence the traditional distinction between theistic proofs as either *a priori* or *a posteriori* is at best misleading and ought to be abandoned. This is not to say, however, that the so-called ontological argument is the only valid argument for God's existence. On the contrary, since the concept of God as itself metaphysical or nothing both implies and is implied by all other metaphysical concepts, not only it but any strictly general concept whatever (actuality, possibility, order, truth, value) can provide the premise of a valid theistic proof, unless theism itself is metaphysically false. And that it is false could be shown only by the same kind of argument, to the effect that any and all of our most basic ideas, including the idea of God, make the existence of God impossible, and this, in the final analysis, because the faith by which we live is in its essence atheistic. Thus there is no complete list, to be made out in advance, of all the possible proofs and disproofs of theism. All we can be certain of is that any properly metaphysical concept, assertion, or chain of reasoning will of necessity have theistic or atheistic implications.

As to the place of proof in philosophical theology, the important point is the essentially derived and secondary function of all reflective understanding, and so, *a fortiori*, of all rational argument. Whitehead comments that "'proof,' in the strict sense of that term, [is] a feeble, second-rate procedure." He does not mean by this that strict rational argument has no place at all in philosophy, for he goes on to say that "'proof' is one of the routes by which self-evidence is often obtained." Thus he concludes: "Proofs are the tools for the extension of our imperfect self-evidence. They presuppose some clarity; and they also presuppose that this clarity represents an imperfect penetration into our dim recognition of the world around—the world of fact, the world of possibility, the world as valued, the world as purposed"

(1938: 66, 69). Here, it seems to me, is the charter for a philosophical theology that neither overestimates the importance of rational argument for God's existence, as is the wont of the *philosophia perennis*, nor simply eliminates such argument, as has so often been done by Protestant theologians since Schleiermacher. The truth cannot lie either in making everything depend on "demonstration" or else in dismissing proof altogether in favor of "insight" and "phenomenological description." The truth, rather, is that "proofs must rest on insights" (Hartshorne, 1941: 59) or, as we may also say, all proofs are but the reflection of existential faith, and so essentially secondary, although for the same reason still important.

In any case, philosophical theology or theistic metaphysics comprises considerably more than the development of "proofs" in the strict sense of the word. The burden of its task, indeed, consists in two main responsibilities that respectively precede and follow any such development.

Its first responsibility, as Antony Flew puts it, is "to begin right from the beginning, with a presentation and examination of the notion of God" (28). This requires, in turn, that it seek to answer two fundamental questions: (1) as to the bases in our common faith and experience for our having any notion of God at all; and (2) as to how this notion may be conceived precisely enough to avoid vagueness, while also avoiding incoherence, either with itself or with our other general conceptions and experience. These two questions are so fundamental that no philosophical theology failing to deal with them could possibly accomplish its task. But they have a particular pertinence and force in our present cultural situation, for which the very notion of God is the problem, either because it is thought to be insufficiently based in our common experience, or because it is held to be incoherent both with itself and with other essential items of our understanding and belief. Ours, in a word, is a postcritical situation which demands that theistic metaphysics begin from the beginning with nothing less than "a methodical-systematic laying of foundations" (Coreth). To ignore this demand by proceeding at once to develop the traditional theistic proofs is to guarantee that philosophical theology itself will be ignored by the one segment of society that has both the competence and the vocation to assess its claims.

And yet not even the laying of foundations for its superstructure of rational argumentation exhausts philosophical theology's task. It has the further responsibility, as Flew puts it, of assessing the "credentials" submitted by "the various candidate systems of revelation" that advance their special claims on a theistic basis (124). Even if it belongs to religion by its very nature to advance such special claims, the fact that it presents them as generally applicable and, in some cases, universally valid means that there have to be at least some reasons correspondingly general or universal for accepting them, if their acceptance is to be at all rationally motivated. It is not surprising, therefore, that the great world religions have commonly adduced such reasons— traditional Christianity, for example, by way of proofs of miracles and of the fulfillment of prophecy and other arguments designed to establish the unique inspiration and authority of the church. Since these reasons are offered as exactly that, as reasons, philosophical theology has both the right and the responsibility to assess their logical and experiential force. Nor can there be any limit to this right and responsibility short of the necessary limit to all attempts at rational justification. So far as any belief or assertion, even a doctrine of religion originating in special revelation, lays claim to universal validity or truth, it both warrants and demands such reflective assessment of its claim as it is possible for human reason to provide.

4. *Precisely as the task of an independent philosophy, philosophical theology is necessarily presupposed by a specifically Christian theology whose task is the fully reflective understanding of Christian faith.*

So formulated, this thesis applies to the special case of Christian theology certain general principles governing the relation between philosophy or philosophical theology and the reflective understanding of any particular religious faith. Such a formulation seems more than justified here because the motives behind this entire undertaking are those of a Christian theologian seeking fuller self-consciousness about his own specific task. Even so, it is important to recognize that the principles involved are not peculiarly Christian but could be applied, *mutatis mutandis*, to any particular religion and theology whatever.

According to the view previously explained, religion in its various expressions is the primary and most direct reflection of the basic existential faith by which we all live simply as human beings. As such, it never exists in general, any more than art or science does, but always exists as *a* religion which has its origin in some particular occasion of insight or special revelation. Correlative with such revelation as the response through which it is received is a particular form of faith, which in turn provides the foundation for a whole structure of beliefs, rites, and social organizations. In many cases (although, admittedly, this is a variable which happens to be especially pronounced in Christianity), this religious structure is eventually subjected to reflective understanding, whereupon a theology of the religion appears on the scene. Naturally, since even the most direct and spontaneous religious expression is itself the product of understanding, it is already to some degree reflective and to that extent theology. But theology strictly so-called is the more sustained, deliberate, and therefore specialized reflection whereby the primary expression of religion is subjected to critical analysis and interpretation.

As such, the theological understanding of a particular religion is obviously similar to what we have previously understood by "philosophy." In fact, we have ample warrant for asserting the following *analogia proportionalitatis*: just as philosophy is the fully reflective understanding of our common faith simply as selves, so Christian theology, say, is the attempt to become fully self-conscious about specifically Christian faith. This assumes, of course, that Christianity is in the formal sense a religion just like any other. But so far from being objectionable, this assumption clearly seems required both by the methods and the conclusions of our best contemporary knowledge and by Christianity's explicit statements about itself.

Having asserted this analogy, however, I would now call attention to its peculiarity—a peculiarity that manifests itself in a number of ways, of which only the more important can be briefly considered.

In the first place, Christianity, being a religion, occupies what Whitehead speaks of as "the peculiar position" of religion, that it stands "between abstract metaphysics and the particular principles applying to only some among the experiences of life" (1926: 31). This being so, Christian theology cannot be regarded as merely one more special science and is not properly called a "science" at all unless it is in its own way absolutely basic and comprehensive. To be sure, it is unlike philosophy in that its origin is not simply in what I call "original revelation," meaning thereby the primal disclosure of reality as such as received somehow through our common faith as selves. Theology originates, rather, in a special revelation which represents its relation to original revelation and to all other special revelations as that of *the* answer to a question. Thus the Johannine Christ is represented as saying, "Truly, truly, I say to you, before Abraham was, I am" (Jn. 8:58). But because of the peculiar nature of this answer, and so, of course, of the question it presupposes, Christian theology as the reflective understanding thereof cannot be less basic or comprehensive than philosophy itself. Hartshorne effectively confirms this when he observes that "religious ideas claim to be the concrete form of ultimate truths. . . . For religious ideas claim absolute ultimacy. They must involve all ultimate truths, which must be deducible from them. Otherwise, secular [*sc.* philosophical] truth would be more final than religious" (1941: 113). In this first important respect, then, Christian theology is not only like philosophy, but also has and must have the same ultimate basis and scope; for the revelation in which it has its origin is, by this revelation's own claim, the decisive re-presentation of God's original revelation to human existence as such, in which philosophy itself originates.

Christian theology is also like philosophy, indeed like all reflection, in being essentially historical. Thus not only is it always a task performed in a particular cultural situation having definite possibilities and limitations, but it can hardly be accomplished save through critico-constructive discussion with the tradition of understanding in which the faith it would reflect has been previously re-presented and reflected. In the first instance, of course, this tradition is what is usually referred to as "the Christian tradition" in the broadest sense of the words, as comprising the beliefs, rites, social organizations, and theology of the Christian religion, as well as the rest of human life and culture so far as historically shaped thereby. As a matter of fact, Christian theology is essentially distinguishable from philosophy in that the faith it seeks to understand is accessible even existentially, thanks only to its mediation by this quite particular tradition. But this is simply to say that theology's dependence on history reflects a still deeper dependence on history, which is based on the fact that the object of theological reflection is itself historically determined. Even so, theology's parallel with philosophy is close both because the evidence to which it attends comprises the whole of the Christian tradition and because it considers the properly theological element in this tradition always to have but secondary evidential force, relative to the more direct witness of the Christian community.

Here again, however, the likeness between Christian theology and philosophy exhibits a peculiarity that makes this likeness more than an ordinary analogy of proportionality. This is evident, first of all, in that theology's preunderstanding is one and the same with philosophy's. By the claim of Christian faith itself, whose witness is addressed to every human being without exception, nothing is required by way of a preunderstanding of the Christian tradition beyond what is already required even for philosophical understanding, namely, the existential faith that constitutes human existence. This means, among other things, that existential affirmation of the Christian faith is not a precondition of theological understanding, even though wherever such affirmation occurs the task of theology is set as an imperative task. But the peculiarity of the analogy also appears from the fact that the evidence to which theological reflection must attend cannot be restricted solely to the specifically Christian tradition, however broadly construed, or for all of its decisive importance. Just as religion in general is not merely coordinate with the other fields of culture but is fundamental to and uniquely representative of them, so any religion claiming to be *the* religion can sustain its claim only if it is somehow expressed or implied by the whole of human life. In the last analysis, then, Christian theology is like philosophy not only in *appealing* to historical evidence but in appealing to the *same* evidence—even if in pursuit of its own distinctive task and thus with the aim of showing that such evidence both confirms and is confirmed by the specifically Christian faith it seeks to understand.

It would be possible to extend this comparative analysis by considering how theology is also like philosophy in having a constructive-synthetic as well as a critico-analytic function—or, as theologians would more likely put it, in being "systematic" as well as "historical." Likewise, we could consider how the task of theological understanding has come to be differentiated his-

torically into several more special tasks, which nevertheless re-
tain their essential unity insofar as they all contribute to the
central responsibility of systematic theology. But extending the
analysis in these ways could only confirm further what should
already be sufficiently clear—that philosophy and Christian theology are not only closely analogous but because of the peculiar
relation between their respective objects, between our basic existential faith and specifically Christian faith, also overlap or in
a certain way coincide.

From this it follows that Christian theology necessarily presupposes philosophy, and this not simply in general or in any
of philosophy's widely different forms, but in the quite particular
form of philosophical theology or theistic metaphysics. Because
theology and philosophy by their very natures finally lay claim
to the same basic ground, appeal to the same historical evidence—in short, serve an identical ultimate truth—their material
conclusions must be in the last analysis mutually confirming if
either is to sustain its essential claim. This does not mean, of
course, that their complete mutual confirmation must be actually
realized, either now or at some time in the future. The essentially
historical character of reflection, not to mention such other con-
stants of the human equation as finitude and sin, hardly permits
this as a real possibility. We simply have to reckon with the indefinite continuation of our present more or less irreducible pluralism of philosophical and theological positions. But in doing
so, we have no reason whatever to set aside the ideal that philosophy and theology alike establish as governing their relation-
ship—even though we have the best of reasons for suspecting
all claims to have already realized this ideal. So long as philosophy is a serious undertaking it involves the confidence, which
it attempts to justify, that the truth of its material conclusions
can only be confirmed by any true conclusions of Christian theology—and theology, naturally, involves and seeks to justify a
corresponding confidence about the confirmation of its conclusions by those of philosophy.

Since our interest here is in theology's relation to philosophy,
we must now consider more closely why the philosophy it presupposes must of necessity be a philosophical theology or a
theistic metaphysics. The basic reason has already been given in
pointing to the peculiar overlapping or coincidence of theological

with philosophical understanding. But this reason can be developed in different ways, each of which is worth considering, even if it is implied by, as well as implies, the others.

One way begins with the observation that, for all the specificity of its origin and object, Christian theology is nevertheless an effort at reflective understanding, and so subject to the conditions of human reflection generally. Thus, for instance, it must seek to avoid the opposite evils of overcoming unclarity only at the price of incoherence and escaping inconsistency only by settling for vagueness. Or it must satisfy the twin demands that its terms and assertions be logically consistent, both with themselves and with one another, and experientially significant in that they are warranted somehow by our actual experience. But underlying all such conditions is the fact that theology is possible at all only in terms of concepts. "Reflective understanding" in the full sense applicable to theology means precisely conceptual understanding. Yet whence is theology to obtain its concepts, if not from philosophy? And what philosophy can provide the kind of conceptuality theology needs except a complete theistic metaphysics?

The implied answers to these questions do not require us to suppose either that theology's dependence on philosophy is always direct or that individual theologians are necessarily dependent on other individuals who are philosophers. It is always possible, indeed likely, that the direct source of a theologian's principal concepts will be the specifically theological tradition in which he or she stands. Even so, if one investigates the provenance of these concepts, one is almost certain to discover the influence of some form of philosophical reflection directly proportional to the clarity and precision that recommend them for theological use. Similarly, it is perfectly possible that the philosophical reflection on which particular theologians are most dependent is precisely their own—that they are, as it were, their own philosophers. And yet if such theologians are wise, they will be sensitive enough to the immense difficulties of their task to be eager for all the help they can get, and thus to maintain the most intensive and extensive discussion possible with their philosopher colleagues. By the same token, they will be particularly keen to learn everything they can from any philosophy that is sufficiently profound and comprehensive to clarify all the concepts necessary to an adequate reflective understanding of Christian faith.

Another way of making the same point proceeds from the fact that Christian theology is nothing if not the most serious possible concern with truth. This concern is so essential to theology not only because, being a form of reflective understanding, it could not fail to be thus concerned, but also, and crucially, because the faith it seeks to understand itself claims to be true. In making this claim, to be sure, Christian faith is no different from religion generally, at least the other world religions, which also make or imply the same kind of claim. But this should only make all the clearer why theology must be centrally concerned with validating the claim as it is advanced by Christian faith.

In this connection, it may be helpful to recall the familiar notion of "the risk of faith." This notion is usually taken to mean that, insofar as Christian faith is an understanding of one's existence to which there are in some sense real alternatives, it involves a choice, and so is in that respect a risk. Specifically, it is the risk that the basic truth of human existence is as it is represented to be in the witness of faith to Jesus Christ that is the Christian special revelation. It follows, then, given the understanding of religion and theology previously developed, that there must be a reflective as well as an existential way of taking this risk, or, in other words, that the reflection of Christian faith in theological assertions is the venture of faith itself at the level of full self-consciousness. But to recognize this is to see once again why Christian theology is necessarily dependent not simply on some philosophy or other, but on an integral theistic metaphysics. For how can the venture of faith be reflectively confirmed, or theology's assertions rationally justified, except on the basis of just such a metaphysics?

To reply, as has often been done, that faith and theology do not need rational justification is either to ignore faith's own claim to be true or else to admit, in effect, that its claim is empty and not to be taken seriously. And this must be said just as emphatically of current versions of the reply, which hold that "there can be no *general* justification of religion," as of its more traditional versions, which maintain simply that faith is "above" reason and, therefore, cannot and need not be validated by it

(Phillips: 72). There is no denying, of course, that philosophers do often exhibit "a craving for generality," and the reminder is insofar pertinent that "the distinction between the real and the unreal does not come to the same thing in every context" (63). But this in no way exempts theology from meeting the essential requirements of cognitive meaningfulness. Hence, while it might be plausibly argued that Christian faith alone is a sufficient ground for the *truth* of theology's assertions, it would be plainly absurd to claim that it suffices to establish their *meaningfulness*. Assertions as a rule can be established as meaningful, and hence as candidates for true belief, only by showing that they refer through at least some possible experience that could serve to verify them. Furthermore, in the case of foundational theological assertions which in their logic are metaphysical, thus to establish their meaningfulness is equivalent to establishing their truth; for either they can be shown to refer through *all* possible experience, or else they are doubtfully meaningful as metaphysical assertions. Thus not only is it evident that Christian faith alone is an insufficient ground for theology's assertions, but it is also clear that such assertions cannot be established as even meaningful except by establishing a theistic metaphysics that is true independently of specifically Christian faith.

Yet a third way of reaching the same conclusion develops the insight that the task of Christian theology is by its very nature hermeneutical. Up to this point, I have been at pains to avoid the term "hermeneutics" and its cognates because they have been so overused that they have tended to become a substitute for careful thinking instead of being its instrument. But I have no reason to deny that the description of theology (and of philosophy, too, for that matter) as a hermeneutical undertaking may be given an exact meaning by the account presented here. On the contrary, according to this account, theology is the reflective understanding of Christian faith and is thus, by direct implication, the critical interpretation of the witness of the Christian community.

But this conception of theology has some interesting implications that are not always recognized by proponents of "theology as hermeneutics." It implies, first of all, that theology must so interpret the witness of faith as to present faith itself as the decisive answer to the religious question of humankind. This implies, in turn, that the theologian must become fully conscious of the structure of this religious question, by understanding in an express, thematic, and conceptually precise way both the question itself and its "tacit presuppositions," including the criterion of the truth of any answer to it that these presuppositions contain. Yet since the religious question can be nothing other than the existential question itself, thus to understand its logical structure, so as to interpret the Christian faith as *the* answer to it, is indistinguishable from working out a complete theistic metaphysics. Consequently, unless such a metaphysics were possible as the only adequate interpretation of our common faith, the task of Christian theology as a hermeneutical task could never be accomplished.

In all these ways, we see why the fully reflective understanding of the Christian faith necessarily presupposes an independent philosophical theology. And it should be just as evident that the independence of philosophical theology is crucial, since it is solely on this condition that Christian theology itself is possible and can accomplish its specific task. This does not mean, of course, that there is no sense at all in which philosophical theology, for its part, is also dependent on Christian reflection. Given the existence of the Christian religion and theology, they automatically become part, though only a part, of that "variety of expression" on which the philosopher is called to meditate. Moreover, we have seen that philosophy and Christian theology are in essence so related that they both serve the same ultimate truth, which implies that the philosopher's efforts to tell this truth are as responsible to the theologian as the theologian's are to the philosopher. Still, philosophy is and must be—for theology's sake as well as its own—independent of theology, in that it has its origin in human existence as such, rather than in human existence as historically determined by Christian faith. It is just insofar as philosophical theology preserves its independence as the full self-consciousness of our common faith as human beings that it both accomplishes its own essential task and also provides the indispensable presupposition of the specifically different task of Christian theology.

And just this specific difference is also at stake in the independence of philosophical theology. Only insofar as it is independent of Christian theology, as the general is of the special, or as the question is of the answer, is Christian theology itself clearly established as something different. Thus, contrary to what may have been inferred from this account, it has by no means collapsed the difference between theology and philosophy. In fact, I have stressed that theology is essentially distinguished from philosophy because the very object of its reflection is determined by a particular history, so that there would not even be any Christian theology save for specifically Christian revelation and faith. At the same time, I have indicated that it is Christian faith itself that sets the task of theological reflection as an imperative task of the Christian community. Because of its own inner nature and dynamic, faith seeks the fullest possible understanding of itself and its claim; and this means, finally, that it seeks a theological understanding. Hence the very faith that accounts for there being any Christian theology at all likewise accounts for theology's necessarily presupposing an independent philosophical theology. And yet the same faith also explains why theology can never be simply identified with philosophy, but abides in its specific difference as Christian faith itself on its way to full self-consciousness.

5

Prolegomena to Practical Theology

Among the perennial questions of Christian systematic theology is the question as to the nature and the task of Christian theology itself. In this connection, the systematic theologian asks about the nature and task not only of systematic theology, but also of historical and practical theology. This is not to say, of course, that historical and practical theologians must look exclusively to their colleagues in systematic theology to tell them who they are and what they ought to do. On the contrary, insofar as they are really theologians, and hence more than merely secular historians or theoreticians of praxis, they themselves have both the right and the responsibility to reflect critically on the nature and task of theology as such as well as of each of its three disciplines. The fact remains, however, that in pursuing such reflection, historical and practical theologians are asking a *systematic*, not a historical or a practical, theological question—just as, in general, it is not a historical task to inquire about the proper task of history or a task of the theory of praxis to ask about the nature of such theory.

With this in mind, I wish to pursue here the question as to the nature and task of practical theology. Since the more general question about the nature and task of theology as such is the constitutive question of what is traditionally called "prolegomena," I have naturally thought to entitle my reflections accordingly. In doing so, however, I would emphasize that limitations of space as well as of competence allow me to offer only a modest contribution to proper prolegomena to practical theology. I shall be content, indeed, if I can indicate simply how the question of practical theology presently arises and how I myself incline to answer it.

For some time now, I have been convinced that practical theology should be understood much more comprehensively than has commonly been the case (see above, pp. 13–15). Because of certain biases evident in the whole tradition of witness and theology, the visible church has been classically defined exclusively in religious and even clerical terms—as it clearly is, for example, in Article XIII of the Articles of Religion of the Methodist Church, when it is said to be "a congregation of faithful men in which the pure Word of God is preached, and the Sacraments duly administered according to Christ's ordinance" (Patterson *et al.* [eds.]: 58). Corresponding to this narrow definition of the church, practical theology has usually been understood simply as more or less critical reflection on the explicit witness of faith through the forms of religion, and this solely in connection with the official functions of the representative ministry. To be sure, from Friedrich Schleiermacher on there has been a growing tendency to identify the visible church as such, instead of the representative minister and the individuals to whom he or she ministers, as the subject and the object of the praxis on which practical theology reflects. To this extent, practical theology has indeed come to be conceived more comprehensively than the merely pastoral theology out of which it emerged (Haendler: 3–10). But it is only in our own time, with the ever clearer relativization of religion in its traditional forms, that the visible church has clearly appeared to comprise more than the explicitly religious and to have the primary object of its witness or praxis in the world it is sent to serve. Consequently, it is really only since the early 1970s that works in practical theology have appeared in which it is understood to be correspondingly comprehensive in scope. Representative in this connection is the understanding of practical theology proposed by Gert Otto, who defines it as "the critical theory of praxis in society that is mediated religiously" (Otto [ed.]: 23; cf. Otto: 75–89).

As much as I can only welcome this development, I cannot deny that it raises a question about the distinctive place of practical theology that neither I nor others sharing a similar understanding have adequately addressed. As long as the praxis on which practical theology has the task of reflecting is conceived to be either merely clerical or merely religious, its difference both from theology in general and from the other disciplines of historical and systematic theology is obvious enough. But this is no longer the case once its object is understood to be all praxis in society that is mediated by the Christian witness, and thus implicit witness through all secular social and cultural forms as well as explicit witness through the forms of religion. As a matter of fact, when practical theology comes to be understood this comprehensively, it hardly seems to have any place at all, as distinct from moral theology or ethics, itself conceived as that part of systematic theology which reflects critically on human existence and action insofar as they are mediated by the Christian witness.

Of course, we ought not to assume uncritically that there simply has to be a distinct discipline of practical theology. Reflection on the nature and task of theology itself, including its differentiation into disciplines, is just as historically conditioned as theological reflection on anything else. Moreover, the differentiation of theology that Protestants today usually take for granted emerged only in the course of the nineteenth century and has been subject to changes ever since. Thus, for example, the ongoing development of historical-critical study of scripture has completely undercut any sharp distinction between scripture and tradition and has thereby called into question the place of biblical, or exegetical, theology as a distinct discipline coordinate with historical, systematic, and practical theology. Recognizing this, we simply have to ask whether or not a similar fate has now overtaken practical theology, given an understanding of its scope as coextensive with all Christian witness or praxis, lay as well as clerical and generally social and cultural as well as specifically religious.

Without considering what might be said for answering this question affirmatively, I want to mention two conditions under either of which it seems to me one might reasonably answer it negatively.

The first such condition is that, even given so comprehensive an understanding of its scope, practical theology's relation to the situation in and for which all theological reflection is done remains distinctively different from that of systematic and, therefore, moral theology. My assumption here, obviously, is that moral and practical theology are alike in that, both being forms of theological reflection, they always take place in and for some particular situation. Because to exist humanly at all is always to exist historically, in a particular society and culture, any form of reflection is historically or situationally conditioned. Thus, however different their respective questions may be, moral and practical theology are alike insofar as they can neither ask nor answer their questions except in the terms of some situation, with its particular problems and resources for solving them. Even so, one may still maintain that moral and practical theology do pursue distinctively different questions, as a result of which their relations to the situation in and for which they reflect are correspondingly different. Whereas moral theology properly asks how one is to exist and act in relation to one's fellow beings in any situation whatever insofar as one understands one's existence in accordance with the Christian witness, practical theology properly asks what one is to do in the particular situation in and for which one must here and now take responsibility if one is to actualize such a Christian self-understanding. Naturally, the only terms in which the moral theologian can answer even his or her distinctive question are those of the particular situation in which he or she must ask it. Nevertheless, the proper object of moral theological reflection is Christian existence and action as such, as distinct from the particular agenda for Christian praxis in the present that is the proper object of practical theology.

A possible objection to this reasoning is that it preserves a distinctive place for practical theology only by implying a narrow understanding of the scope of moral theological concern. Certainly, if one judges from what moral theologians typically think and say, they are concerned with the particular responsibilities of Christian praxis here and now as well as with the general principles of Christian existence and action in all situations. But even if one allows this to be the case, and so rejects any narrow understanding of moral theology, one may still insist on its difference from practical theological reflection.

In a broad sense of the word, all theological reflection, in any of the three disciplines, is "practical," in that it is reflection on the Christian witness as decisive for human existence and, therefore, also for human praxis. Consequently, moral theologians, also, are and must be concerned in their way with the present responsibilities of Christian praxis; and to this extent there is an important overlap of their concern with that of their colleagues in practical theology. Nevertheless, one may hold that moral theologians are concerned with present praxis in *their* way rather than in the distinctively different way of practical theologians. Their way of being concerned with such praxis is to formulate the general principles by which all Christian praxis is more or less fully determined, and any account they may give of the present situation is simply by way of formulating these principles.

In this respect, there is a close analogy to the difference between systematic, including moral, theology and the third discipline of historical theology. If all theology is in a broad sense "practical," all theology is also in a broad sense "historical"— and for essentially the same reason. Because all theology is reflection on the Christian witness as decisive for human existence, systematic theologians are and must be as concerned as historical theologians with the past traditions of such witness. Even so, their way of being thus concerned is distinctively different from that of their historical theologian colleagues. They are concerned with past traditions insofar as they formulate the general principles of existence and belief to which all Christian tradition more or less adequately bears witness, and any account they may give of any past situation is simply by way of formulating these principles.

I conclude, therefore, that, even when moral theology is understood comprehensively, as being concerned with present praxis as well as with general principles, practical theology might still be held to have a place, provided only that its relation to the present is as distinctively different from that of systematic theology as is historical theology's relation to the past.

The second condition under which one might reasonably draw the same conclusion is that, even when the scope of practical theology is understood to extend to all kinds of Christian witness or praxis, lay as well as clerical and generally social and cultural as well as specifically religious, the aspect under which practical theology reflects on witness or praxis is distinctively different from that under which moral theology reflects on it. What I have in mind here can be brought out by comparing a similar position that was already advanced in the nineteenth century by C. D. F. Palmer, in what must surely be one of the most penetrating essays on practical theology ever written (Palmer; cf. Rössler). In Palmer's opinion, the dominant understanding of practical theology after Schleiermacher, which tended to assimilate it to that part of systematic theology that the German tradition distinguishes as "dogmatics," did not bode at all well for the future of the discipline. By understanding it, in effect, as the critical and normative theory of the church, most theologians not only compromised its identity as distinct from dogmatics but, even worse, made it entirely a matter of formulating general principles without any immediate concern for problems of praxis. Troubled by these consequences, Palmer made the innovative proposal that the understanding of practical theology be oriented, not to dogmatics, but to the other part of systematic theology that the Germans call "ethics" and that I have spoken of here as "moral theology." Such an orientation is appropriate, he contended, because practical theology and ethics both employ the same basic method and both have to do with the same encompassing theme: human life under the conditions of Christianity. At the same time, Palmer was concerned about the difference between the two forms of reflection and took pains to see that they were clearly distinguished. Whereas ethics or moral theology, he argued, reflects on "*Christian* life," in the sense of the life to be lived by each believer as an individual person, practical theology has as its object "*ecclesial* life," in the sense of the shape to be given to the life of the church (327; italics added).

It is just here, however, that Palmer's proposal revealed a serious weakness. In thus distinguishing between the Christian and the church, he showed himself to share the traditional bias according to which the church as such is defined exclusively in religious terms. Thus when he went on to specify the several "practical theories" that he took to be of the essence of practical theology, it is significant that the only such theories he explicitly mentioned—e.g., homiletics, catechetics, and liturgics—all had to do with the specifically religious (323, 349, 352, 355, 359). Consequently, as innovative as his proposal certainly was in understanding practical theology primarily in relation to moral theology, it perpetuated an understanding of the church and of the scope of practical theology that we have now come to think of as too restricted.

The question I wish to raise, however, is whether something

like the same distinction between the Christian and the church cannot still be made even with an understanding of the church as more than merely religious. Suppose one holds, as I do, that the visible church as such is constituted, not by word and sacraments and special ministry, but by the Christian witness of faith of which word and sacraments and special ministry are representative forms. Suppose one further holds, as I also do, that the witness of faith that constitutes the church comprises not only explicit witness through religious forms but also implicit witness through all the secular forms of society and culture. On these suppositions, then, one may claim, as I do, that the visible church as such is present in the witness, implicit and explicit, of each individual Christian and that the only constitutive ministry in the church is the general ministry exercised by all who bear this witness. But if, to this extent, there neither is nor can be an adequate distinction between the Christian and the church, a difference still remains between the witness of faith by which the visible church as such is constituted and the representative forms of this witness like word and sacraments and special ministry. Moreover—and this is the essential point—there are representative forms of the *implicit* witness of faith as well as of the explicit witness of faith, as is clear from the fact that Christians as such are represented not only by sanctuaries and schools of theology but also by hospitals and universities. But this means, then, that, even when the church is conceived radically as the community of faith and witness, and hence as more than merely religious, one still has reason for distinguishing with traditional theology between "the church as a whole" (*ecclesia synthetica*) and "the representative church" (*ecclesia repraesentativa*). This is so, at any rate, if one is also willing to insist against the theological tradition that the witness of the church as a whole which the representative church is supposed to represent comprises not only the explicit witness of cult but the implicit witness of culture as well.

If this reasoning is sound, however, there are evidently two distinct aspects under which Christian witness or praxis can be made the object of theological reflection. It can be reflected on either under the aspect of the church as a whole, and thus of the witness or praxis required of each individual Christian, or else under the aspect of the representative church, and thus of the special forms of witness or praxis whereby the visible church as such is in turn represented. Assuming that on some understandings, at least, reflection under the first aspect might well be assigned to moral theology, one might still see a distinct task for practical theology, provided only that reflection under the second aspect is assigned to it.

Consequently, I incline to think that, under the second of these conditions if not the first, one can answer the question of practical theology as it arises today even while still claiming a distinctive place for it among the disciplines of Christian theology.

6

Theology and Religious Studies: Their Difference and the Difference It Makes

1

The aim of this study is to extend the range of alternatives for dealing with a problem with which Christian theologians today are well acquainted. Accordingly, the word "theology" is used throughout the discussion, not in the generic sense in which we often need to use it, but in the specific sense expressed by the phrase "Christian theology." That this entails a corresponding restriction of the relevance of the discussion, however, is far from obvious; for there is reason to believe that, just as the problem itself is not peculiar to Christian theology, so the discussion of alternative ways of dealing with it also has a wider bearing.

The problem at its core is a perennial theological problem, since among the questions that theology must always ask and answer is the question, What is theology? In this, as in other important respects, theology is very much like philosophy, as distinct from history, the special sciences, and the various arts, none of which bears philosophy's responsibility for critically constituting itself as a distinct form of reflection. Since theology is a form of reflection that, for all of its dependence on a particular history, is and must be as basic and as comprehensive as philosophy, it always bears the same responsibility for critically understanding itself and reflectively establishing the necessary conditions of its own possibility. But what makes this perennial responsibility particularly problematic today is the evident incompatibility between theology's conventional self-understanding and what are now widely accepted as standards of reflection. Indeed, the very claims that theologians usually insist on in establishing the necessary conditions of theological reflection raise the profoundest doubts about its legitimacy, given current standards of what any form of reflection is supposed to be.

These claims are mainly two: (1) that theology as such has to appeal to special criteria of truth for some if not all of its assertions; and (2) that the theologian as such has to be a believer already committed to the truth of the assertions that theological reflection seeks to establish. According to all the usual answers to the question of what theology is, it is necessary to insist on one or both of these claims if theology is to be critically constituted as a distinct form of reflection. And yet to insist on either claim is to run into contemporary counterclaims with respect to what alone can count as legitimate reflection. According to such counterclaims, no form of reflection appealing to special criteria of truth can to this extent be legitimate, since no assertion can possibly be established as true except by appealing to completely general criteria applicable to any other assertion of the same logical type. And even more obvious, according to the same contemporary standards, is the illegitimacy of any form of reflection requiring anyone engaging in it already to believe the assertions that reflection alone can critically establish, as distinct from being able and willing to ask the question to which all such assertions are the answer. On the other hand, to accede to such counterclaims to the point of abandoning both of the claims on which theologians are wont to insist is, from the standpoint of their insistence, to deny the very conditions necessary to theology's being a distinct form of human reflection.

In its logical structure, then, the problem before us is a special case of the dilemma with which theology today is commonly supposed to be confronted. If its self-understanding as theology succeeds in being appropriate to the Christian witness of faith—in that it understands itself to be a form of reflection distinct from every other—it cannot at the same time understand itself in terms of contemporary standards of reflection. If, on the contrary, its self-understanding succeeds in being credible to human existence today—in that it does understand itself in terms of these standards—it cannot also understand itself to be a distinct form of reflection. Because, either way, it is impossible to satisfy both of the demands that an adequate theological self-understanding must satisfy, neither of the usual alternatives for dealing with the problem offers anything like a real solution.

There is a particular formulation of this dilemma on which I now want to focus attention. This is the formulation according to which any theology that understands itself in terms of current standards of reflection cannot at the same time make good the claim to be different from religious studies. Conversely, this formulation holds that any theology that makes good its claim to be different from religious studies can do so only by insisting on at least one of the two claims that are incompatible with such current standards, which is to say, either that theology must appeal at some point to special criteria of truth to establish its assertions or that the theologian must believe these assertions to be true even before seeking to establish them. That this kind of reasoning is commonly expressed or implied in theological discussions of our problem will be acknowledged at once by anyone familiar with them. But what I find just as significant is the extent to which the same reasoning appears in discussions of religious studies by students of religion as well. When such students attempt to explain how their own form of reflection differs from that distinctive of theology, they usually present this difference as primarily if not exclusively negative, in that certain conditions taken to be necessary to the possibility of theology are held not to be necessary to the possibility of religious studies. Specifically, they present religious studies as different from theology mainly because religious studies require no appeal to special criteria to establish their assertions as true and because they require no prior belief in the truth of their assertions from the student of religion.

It is not surprising, of course, that students of religion should commonly understand their form of reflection in this negative way. For it is mainly by differentiating itself from theology, and hence by defining itself over against theology's conventional self-definition, that the field of religious studies has gradually established itself as a distinct field. Even so, theologians have long since ceased to be alone in reasoning as though there are only two clear-cut alternatives for dealing with our problem. Students of religion, also, enforce the supposition that we must choose, finally, between a theology that is really different from religious studies only because it also fails to comply with current standards of reflection and a theology that is in full compliance with such standards only because its difference from religious studies is merely verbal and so does not really make any difference.

My conviction is that these are not the only alternatives between which one may reasonably choose and that the supposed dilemma, consequently, is merely that. Accordingly, my purpose in the following discussion is to provide an account of the difference between theology and religious studies other than the conventional theological account. Since it is just this conventional account that generates both of the usual alternatives for dealing with our problem, to show, as I hope to do, that it is not the only account that can be given is to point the way of escape between the horns of the supposed dilemma. This is so, at any rate, if, on the revisionary account I hope to provide, the difference between the two fields really does make a difference even when theology, no less than religious studies, is so understood as to comply fully with contemporary standards of reflection.

2

The main task now before us is to clarify what is properly understood by "religious studies." I take it that this phrase is now used as widely as it is because many of us have come to prefer speaking of "religious studies" rather than simply "religion" in designating the departments of which we are members. "Department of Religion" tends to convey pretty much the same meaning to many persons as "Department of Theology," and yet most of us are convinced that it properly has a different meaning that somehow needs to be expressed. A department or school of theology may very well teach theology rather as a department of biology teaches biology, or a department of physics teaches physics. But a department of religion is not in business to teach religion but exists, rather, to teach what can be learned and taught *about* religion as itself the object of a certain kind of study or studies, somewhat as living things are the object of biology, or natural things generally are the object of physics. Consequently, the phrase "religious studies" recommends itself to us as more likely to convey what our departments in the college or university are all about.

And yet it is interesting that the phrase we use is "religious studies," not "studies of religion." Of course, to speak of the Department of Studies of Religion would be sufficiently awkward to provide a plausible explanation of our not doing so. But perhaps we speak as we do because we are also aware that not every study that somehow has religion as its object need be the kind of study that our departments properly exist to carry on. To decide this issue, however, requires that we look more closely at the meaning of "religious studies" by way of summary clarifications of both of its constitutive terms, "religion" and "study."

The starting point for both clarifications is a general observation about human existence—namely, that to be human at all is both to live by faith and to seek understanding. For our immediate purpose, which is to clarify what is properly meant by "religion," it is the first part of this observation that is important.

The faith to which I refer in observing that each of us lives by faith is our basic confidence or assurance simply as human beings that life is worth living. To live in any case, even as an animal, is the same as accepting one's life in its larger setting and adjusting oneself to it. This is why George Santayana goes so far as to speak of "animal faith," meaning thereby the inalienable confidence of all animal life in its environment as generally permissive of its struggle to live and to reproduce its kind (Santayana). In the case of the human animal, however, vitality is not only expressed in the sphere of mind or consciousness, but is also raised to the still higher level of spirit, of reflective understanding or self-consciousness. Consequently, human acceptance of life and adjustment to it can no longer be merely instinctive but must be a matter of free and responsible consent. We cannot merely live our life but must, as we say, lead it; and this means that we can live and act, finally, only according to certain principles of truth, beauty, and goodness that we understand to be normative for our existence. Necessarily implied by this understanding is the confidence or assurance that these norms have unconditional validity and that a life lived in accordance with them is truly worth living. In this sense, our experience of ourselves and of our fellow beings in relation to reality as a whole is always essentially an experience grounded in faith. We are selves at all only because of our inalienable trust that our own existence and existence generally are somehow justified and made meaningful by the whole to which we know ourselves to belong.

I do not mean by this that the faith by which we live is necessarily authentic or that the beliefs through which it finds expression can only be true. Such an inference can be made, I think, only because we often fail to make certain necessary distinctions. We assume uncritically that "faith" is to be understood in a wholly positive or eulogistic sense as referring solely to true or authentic faith—rather as we often take "worth" to mean only good, or "value," exclusively positive value. But this assumption, natural and understandable as it may be, restricts our grasp of all that "faith" means and implies. Even a false or inauthentic faith is not simply the absence of faith but is faith itself in its negative mode—somewhat as evil is the negative mode of worth, or disvalue is the negative mode of value. And this, of course, is why an animal lacking in the distinctively human capacity of reflective consciousness not only could not believe in the human way, but could not disbelieve in this way, either. On the other hand, given animals endowed with this capacity, or in other words, given human beings such as ourselves, faith in some mode is not an option but a necessity. We unavoidably live by faith because we exist understandingly or reflectively, because we can exist at all only by somehow consenting to our own existence and to existence as such in confident trust.

This is not to imply, however, that such trust may be simply taken for granted as in no way problematic. Even though we have no alternative, finally, but to trust somehow that life is worth living—everything we think, say, or do necessarily implying such a trust—how exactly we are to understand our faith is so far from being unproblematic as to be continually called into question. The reason for this, generally speaking, is that our life is perforce lived under conditions that threaten to undermine any naive assurance we may have as to its final worth. There are the inescapable facts that we must suffer and die, that we involve ourselves in guilt, and that all our undertakings are exposed to the workings of chance. Or again, there is the loneliness that comes over us in even the most intimate of human relationships and, still worse, the gnawing of doubt and the threat of final meaninglessness when we recognize, as we must, that our most basic beliefs are just the ones of whose truth we must be the least certain at the level of explicit belief. To be sure, none of these conditions would pose the kind of problem it does for us but for our prior assurance that it has been given to us to live and that to do so is, after all, worthwhile. This is why the question of faith, to which religious concepts and symbols in one way or another offer an answer, is never the question *whether* there is a ground of basic confidence in life's worth— any more than the question answered by a properly scientific assertion is *whether* there is a world of fact somehow sufficiently ordered that our experiences in the past and present warrant our having certain expectations for the future. Rather, the question of faith is always *how* the ground of confidence can be so conceived and symbolized that our consent to life can be true and authentic—just as the question of science is always *how* we are to understand the *de facto* order that the world necessarily has, so that we can not only survive in it but also prosper. Nevertheless, the negativities of our existence, if we reflect on them, profoundly challenge our basic confidence and drive us beyond any simple understanding of it. In this way, the conditions of life as we unavoidably live it create the profound need for *re-*assurance, for an understanding of ourselves and the world in relation to reality as a whole that will enable us to make sense of the basic faith we inevitably have.

It is to just this need to make sense somehow of our basic faith in the ultimate worth of life that religion is the response. All the various religions, including what I do not hesitate to call "the Christian religion," are so many attempts under the pressure of this need to solve the problem of understanding our basic faith, given the negativities of our existence. Thus the Christian symbols of resurrection and immortality, for example, evidently function to provide the necessary reassurance as to the ultimate meaning of life, given enough reflection on the boundary situation of death and transience to shatter any naive assurance that life is worth living. How different religions, in particular, provide such reassurance, or with what radicality of insight, is historically variable, depending on which of the conditions of human existence are taken to focus the problem and on the depth at which these conditions are grappled with and understood. Even so, the end of any religion, properly so-called, is so to conceive and symbolize the great inescapabilities of life as to solve the problem of our existence as such: the problem of having to believe somehow in the ultimate worth of life under conditions that make such a faith seem all but impossible.

Thus as I use the terms, "faith" and "religion" are not simply equivalent. In the relatively strict sense in which I speak of it, religion is not identical with our basic faith in the worth of life but is to be distinguished from it as its primary explicit expression in meaningful symbols—specifically, in beliefs, rites, and forms of social organization that together provide a particular answer to the question of the ultimate meaning of our life, or to what I have otherwise spoken of as the question of faith. Accordingly, on my usage, Paul Tillich's famous statement that religion is the substance of culture, while culture is the form of religion has to be reformulated so that it is *faith* which is the substance of culture, while religion is the particular cultural form in which this substance is first of all made explicit (Tillich, 1959; cf. H. R. Niebuhr).

So understood, religion is one form of culture among others and yet, for all that, unique. Since it is the primary explication of the basic faith implicitly presupposed by all the other cultural forms, it is in its own way basic to the whole of human existence, and hence is more than merely coordinate in importance with these other forms. This bears underscoring because one of the illusions fostered by the modern differentiation of culture is that religion is simply one more activity alongside others, having its own special field and its own peculiar ways of cultivating this field.

This understanding seems to have the merit of taking the term "religion" more in the sense in which it is ordinarily understood both by common sense and by the historical, scientific, and philosophical understanding of religion, as over against the use that has become characteristic of apologetic theologians bent on making a case for the Christian or some other religion in a secularized world. At the same time, the clarification I have suggested understands "religion" in a functional sense sufficiently formal to include cultural forms or movements that others, assuming a nonfunctional, or substantive, understanding, would speak of as, at most, "quasi-religions," or possibly "religion surrogates." Thus Communism, for instance, might be quite properly spoken of as a religion in my sense, provided only that it is taken to be not only a certain understanding of our basic faith but also a whole symbolic structure of beliefs, rites, and social organizations whereby such understanding is expressed and enforced—in short, provided that it is taken to be the primary cultural form through which certain men and women today have come to understand their basic human faith.

There are two further points more or less clearly implied by what has been said. The first is that religion never exists in general, any more than any other form of culture does, but always only as *a* religion, which has its origin and principle in some particular occasion of insight, be it "hierophany" or "revelation." Correlative with this originating occasion of insight, then, is a particular form of faith, or understanding of existence, which in turn provides the foundation for a whole symbolic structure of beliefs, rites, and social organizations. How this structure is elaborated and how differentiated it becomes from other forms of culture are, again, open to wide historical variations, as is the extent to which the claims it expresses and implies may eventually be subjected to the higher level of reflection that is properly called "theology" in the generic sense of this word. In any event, the only thing directly accessible to us when we speak of "religion" is some particular religion or religions, some particular way or ways of conceiving and symbolizing ourselves and our world in relation to the mystery encompassing our existence. Consequently, even the true religion, if there be such a thing, could not be identified with religion in general or simply as such. It could only be one particular religion among others, distinguished from all the rest solely by the unique adequacy with which its particular concepts and symbols answered to the need that each religion exists to meet.

The second point is that a particular religion can answer to this need only because or insofar as the determinative use of its concepts and symbols is broadly cognitive. Whatever else a religion is or involves, it crucially is or involves conceptualizing and symbolizing a comprehensive understanding of human existence that claims to be true. To be sure, a religion is not the same as a metaphysics that pursues the question of the ultimate whole of reality in itself in abstraction from the question of the meaning of this reality for us. On the contrary, religious concepts and symbols are rightly said to be "existential" precisely because they express claims about the whole of reality only by also opening up our own possibilities of self-understanding in relation to it. Thus such concepts and symbols typically function not only indicatively, to express assertions, but also expressively, to convey feelings and convictions, and imperatively, to enjoin others to certain beliefs or actions. But as important as it is to recognize their existential function, to ignore that religious concepts and symbols also function metaphysically to assert or imply that certain things are ultimately the case is to make it impossible to explain how they could meet the need they clearly exist to meet. I take it that Clifford Geertz intends to make this same point when he observes that "the empirical differentia of religious activity or religious experience would not exist" if religious symbols did not formulate "a basic congruence between a particular style of life and a specific (if, most often, implicit) metaphysic" (642, 652).

Assuming that "religion" has now been clarified sufficiently for our purposes, we may turn to the second term, "study," by recalling the other part of my initial anthropological observation. Just as we are beings who perforce live by faith, so we are also beings who of necessity seek understanding. Of course, a clear implication of what I have said about our living by faith is that we already have understanding before we ever seek it. Moreover, the basic process of acculturation by which alone any of us ever becomes human is one and the same with the process by which we come to understand ourselves and our world in a certain way—namely, by internalizing the norms of truth, goodness, and beauty objectified in the language and culture in which we are reared. Normally, this also includes internalizing the religion, or the particular understanding of basic faith, typical of this same cultural tradition. Yet we even more obviously internalize the stock of empirical knowledge and skills available to our society, or to our own social class location within it.

But while we thus always already have some understanding both of the ultimate whole of reality revealed by our basic faith and of the natural and human world disclosed through our particular experiences, it is also true that we do and must seek more understanding than we already have. We learn only too soon that much that *appears* to be the case is not really the case at all and that the same is true of much that is *said* to be the case by our fellows in society. Unexpected experiences force revisions in our stock of empirical knowledge and skills, and the need to bring our basic norms to bear in novel situations, or the realization that the norms themselves are controversial and in need of justification, drives us to seek yet a deeper understanding even of them. More important still, understanding is both the *sine qua non* of the distinctively human way of living and also the necessary condition of the distinctively human way of living abundantly. Consequently, since the art of life, as Alfred North Whitehead says, is not only to live, but to live well and to live better, the function of understanding in its service of the art of life is to seek by way of reflection more and better understanding than any we already have so that we may not only survive but prosper (1929: 4, 8). This remains true even if we recognize, as I believe we must, that disinterested reflection for its own sake is one of the constitutive elements in that more abundant life, the quest for which is the underlying motivation of our search for understanding.

It is in this eminently pragmatic context that all the forms of reflection—systematic and historical as well as practical—originate. Simply because of our nature and situation as human beings, we both can and must ask, What is really the case? in all the main ways constitutive not only of the various arts such as law, medicine, engineering, and education, but also of philosophy and the special sciences, natural and human, as well as of history. Moreover, we have two controlling purposes in asking this reflective question in the different ways in which we can and must ask it: (1) to get answers to our questions for the sake of the answers, for which we always have a more or less urgent need; and (2) to get answers to the questions for the sake of asking the questions themselves more effectively—whether in order to secure still more adequate answers than we would otherwise obtain or in order to realize as fully as possible our distinctively human capacity for such reflection. This second purpose is further reinforced by the awareness that gradually emerges in history that all answers are really only ways of formulating questions, anyhow. Because even the most reflective human understanding can never be more than fragmentary, the gap between our subjective understanding and the reality that is its object is never closed; and haunted by the awareness that this is so, we are driven to persist in asking our questions.

What is properly meant by "study" is the reflective effort at further understanding that originates under these basic conditions, which is to say, in our capacity for more adequate understanding than we already have, in the situation that drives us to seek such understanding, and with these two controlling purposes in seeking it. Thus the end of all study is more adequate understanding, and this for the sake, finally, of a more abundant human life. But what is distinctive of any study, properly so-called, is how it pursues this end—namely, deliberately, methodically, and in a reasoned way. Whatever the form of the reflective question—historical, systematic, or practical—it constitutes a proper study only insofar as it is asked intentionally and in accordance with a definite procedure and insofar as any answer given to it is supported by reasoned argument.

This would seem to indicate, then, that if what are referred to as "religious studies" are properly so designated, they can only be so many ways of seeking just such a reflective understanding of what is really the case about religion, to the end, finally, of a fuller realization of our distinctive possibilities as human beings. But this is to return to the issue raised earlier whether this necessary condition of properly speaking of "religious studies" is also a sufficient condition. Is any deliberate, methodical, and reasoned pursuit of the question, What is really the case about religion?, a religious study in the proper sense of the words?

That it is quite properly spoken of as a study of religion seems clear enough. And yet it is just as clear that such a study not only may be but frequently is undertaken in several fields, none of which has religion as its constitutive object of study. Thus sociology and psychology, as well as philosophy and history, normally involve the study of religion, because, given their own constitutive questions as forms of reflection, religion in one way or another falls within the horizon of their fields of inquiry. But what clearly decides the issue against allowing that any study of religion is *eo ipso* a religious study is that religion itself is crucially a matter of answering one form of the reflective question as to what is really the case. Because religion exists, as I have argued, to give answer to the question of faith by expressing a comprehensive understanding of our existence in relation to ultimate mystery, the only study of religion as such, and, in this sense, religious study, is some way or other of reflectively understanding religion as an answer to this question of faith. In other words, if the constitutive question of religious studies is, What is really the case about religion?, this is so only because or insofar as this question is understood to ask about the meaning and truth of religion as itself a claim to truth.

To be sure, experience confirms in fact what is already evident in principle, that to ask and answer this question is to constitute not one but several forms of study—historical and practical as well as systematic. And this explains why the sociology of religion is not a concern only of sociologists, or the philosophy of religion, only of philosophers. But what makes any such study of religion a constituent part of religious studies, as distinct from some other field such as sociology or philosophy, is that it is itself constituted by, and in some way contributes toward answering, this one reflective question as to the meaning and truth of religion, given our universally human question about the ultimate meaning of our life.

Assuming now that there is this difference between religious studies as such and all other studies of religion, exactly what kind of a difference is it? As I have just indicated, the sociology of religion is a concern of students of religion as well as of sociologists, and the same may be said, *mutatis mutandis*, of the philosophy of religion, the psychology of religion, and so on. But this is to say that it is the same sociology of religion, philosophy of religion, and so on, that is and must be of concern to students in both of the respective fields, because or insofar as it is a study that springs from the same intention, proceeds by the same method, and judges by the same criteria. However different the questions ultimately constituting some form of study as a constituent part of different fields, it is immediately constituted by the question that it exists to ask and answer; and it is this question, rather than the questions constituting the different fields, that determines its task, method, and criteria.

The difference of religious studies, then, does not entail any difference in the criteria of truth of constituent parts of the field as compared with those of studies of religion generally. Nor is there any reason to suppose otherwise simply because one insists, as I have, that religious studies are constituted as a distinct form of reflection by the question as to the meaning and truth of religion. For even if the criteria of religious truth are sufficiently different from those of other fields of inquiry to be judged *sui generis*, this can only be the judgment of the same philosophy of religion that is as much a concern of philosophers as of students of religion.

If the difference of religious studies in no way implies their having special criteria of truth, however, it just as little implies that the student of religion as such must already be religious. True, I have implied by my account that the student of religion in the strict sense in which I have been using the phrase must be able and willing to ask the question of faith to which religion exists to provide the answer; and if such ability and willingness are taken to be sufficient conditions of being "religious," then, of course, the student of religion must already be so. But on my use of the term and, as I have explained, on what I take to be the use both of common sense and of serious study, such conditions are not sufficient but only necessary conditions of being religious, religion itself not being constituted except by some *answer* to the question of faith, and hence neither by the question itself nor by the basic confidence underlying it. Consequently, I see no good reason to suppose that the student of religion as such needs to be any more religious than the sociologist or the philosopher, who are also, in their ways, students of religion. The only qualification required of either kind of student is the ability and willingness to ask the question constitutive of his or her respective field of study; and in the one case no less than in the other this question arises quite naturally in any human existence that is sufficiently reflective.

The conclusion seems warranted, then, that, since the difference of religious studies entails neither special criteria for their assertions nor special qualifications of their students, it would remain even if one were to deny both of these possible grounds for claiming it, being sufficiently accounted for solely by the question that constitutes them a single field of study. Because any religious study is ultimately constituted as such by the question as to the meaning and truth of religion, this question alone not only unites it with every other religious study but also differentiates it from all other forms of reflection, including even such studies of religion as are ultimately constituted by other questions. But if the question constituting religious studies itself suffices to ground their difference, there can be no doubt about its really making a difference. For even the same form of study, having the identical task, method, and criteria, becomes significantly different contingently upon being ultimately constituted by the question of religious studies, as distinct, say, from the question constituting sociology. In the one case the whole point of the study is to contribute somehow toward answering the question as to the regularities exhibited by human life in society; in the other, the very same study, pursued by persons having no different qualifications and judging by no different criteria, has the very different point of somehow increasing our understanding of the meaning and truth of religion. In short, the question constituting religious studies makes them all really and not merely verbally different from every other because it makes them all constituent parts of a single field-encompassing field whose own difference from every other is indubitably real.

3

The claim I now wish to urge is that one can provide a strictly analogous account of the difference of theology as a field of study from religious studies. By "theology" here I mean, naturally, specifically Christian theology. But just what is meant by the term in this specific sense?

One may say that in its generic sense, which corresponds to the generic sense of "religion," "theology" designates a higher level of reflection to which the claims of a particular religion may possibly be subjected. This would seen to indicate that "theology" in the specific sense of "*Christian* theology" must be reflection on the claims expressed or implied by the *Christian* religion—or, as one might prefer to say, the Christian witness of faith, seeing that religion is not the only, even if the most explicit, primary form of culture through which Christian faith both can and should bear witness. Assuming that such reflection could be properly called a study, we could further infer that theology must consist in asking in a deliberate, methodical, and reasoned way, What is really the case about the Christian religion or witness of faith? Finally, recognizing that the Christian religion, like every other, is constituted by an explicit answer to the question of faith—this same answer being attested implicitly by all other forms of Christian witness—we could conclude that theology must so understand its question as to ask about the meaning and truth of the Christian religion as itself a claim to truth.

Thus to understand theology, however, is obviously to raise the issue of its difference from religious studies. For if theology is, in effect, study of the Christian religion so as to answer the reflective question as to its meaning and truth, the same may also be said of religious studies, at least on the account I have given here and assuming only that, as study of the meaning and truth of religion generally, they surely must include such study of the Christian religion in particular. Moreover, the fact that the object of theology's study is not only the Christian religion as such but all forms of implicit Christian witness as well is not sufficient to establish any difference. For it is not only the Christian religion but, as we have seen, any religion that expresses a faith implicitly attested by all other cultural forms; and so religious studies themselves must have as much reason as theology could have to study the Christian religion only in the context of the Christian witness of faith through culture generally. Is this to imply, then, that the difference of theology from religious studies is merely verbal, because any study of the Christian religion so as to determine its meaning and truth is *eo ipso* theology in the proper sense of the word?

Clearly, the question is analogous to the one asked earlier about any study of religion already being properly a religious study. But as I have indicated, my conviction is that it may also be given an analogous answer, and this means, of course, a negative answer. Even though religious studies themselves certainly can and should inquire about the meaning and truth of the Christian religion, provided that it exists and can be the object of their study, the very fact that we must add this provision reminds us that they are in no way constituted as a field by the question as to the meaning and truth of this particular religion— any more, say, than a sociology that certainly can and should ask about religion generally is constituted as such by the question as to the meaning and truth of religion. The pertinent question, in other words, is not whether the Christian religion with its claim to truth is *also* an object of religious studies, which it plainly is, but, rather, whether it is their *constitutive* object, the object inquiry about which constitutes them as a distinct field of study. The answer to this question, however, is perfectly clear, since the existence of the Christian religion as such is not in the least among the necessary conditions of the possibility of the field of religious studies. It would, or at any rate could, exist as a distinct field of study whether or not the Christian religion or any other particular religion existed, provided only that there were at least some human beings who were religious in one way or another and there was someone both able and willing to pursue the question as to the meaning and truth of their particular religion.

And yet it is just as clear that theology as such would not even be possible except for the prior existence of the Christian witness of faith—assuming, at least, that it is precisely this witness that is theology's constitutive object. But we are entitled to make this assumption if, as I maintain, theology not only asks the question as to the meaning and truth of this particular witness but is constituted as such precisely by doing so—analogously to the way in which religious studies not only ask about the meaning and truth of religion generally but could not exist as such but for asking this question.

Of course, in the case of theology, also, to ask its constitutive question is to constitute not one but several forms of study, as is evident not only from the very meaning of the question itself but also from the actual organization of the field as a whole into the three main disciplines of historical, systematic, and practical theology. And again, this explains why there is considerable overlapping between theology and one or more religious studies or studies of religion generally—in that the history of Christianity, say, is not a concern only of students of religion or historians, or the meaning of the concept "God" is not a concern only of philosophers of religion or philosophical theologians. But an analogous rule also applies here insofar as what makes any such study of Christianity or of the concept "God" a constituent part of theology—as distinct from some other field such as religious studies or philosophy—is that it is itself constituted by, and in some way contributes toward answering, the question of theology: the reflective question as to the meaning and truth of the Christian witness as an answer to our own question of faith as human beings.

Because in theology's case also, however, the ground of its difference as a field of study is precisely its constitutive question, its difference from religious studies would remain even if one were to deny both that it requires special criteria for its assertions and that it requires special qualifications of theologians. This is because there is as little reason here as in the analogous case of religious studies to suppose that the different question theology as such is constituted to ask entails either a difference in the criteria of truth of its constitutent disciplines, as compared with those of cognate fields of study, or else that the theologian as such must already believe in the truth of the Christian witness of faith.

Even if the whole point of historical theology, for example, is to contribute in some way toward increasing our understanding of the meaning and truth of just this witness of faith, it is in no way required to judge by different criteria of truth from those appealed to in the history of religions and history generally. As a matter of fact, it could not appeal to any different criteria and still make its proper contribution to the inquiry of the field as a whole. The same is true even of systematic theology, which directly asks the question of the truth of the Christian witness. It need in no way appeal to special criteria to judge the truth of this particular witness and, in fact, dare not do so if it is to be at all appropriate to the universal claim of this witness itself.

It is just as certain that one does not have to be a Christian believer before one can ask and answer theology's constitutive question. Here, too, the only necessary conditions of asking and answering this question are the prior existence of its constitutive object and of some subject able and willing to ask about this object. But the sufficient ground of there being such a subject in the case of theology's question is there being someone able and willing to ask the question of faith; and since one becomes a Christian not merely by asking this universal question but only by giving a specific answer to it, being a Christian clearly is not among the necessary conditions of being a theologian.

The supposition is plainly false, then, that theology could make good its claim to be different from religious studies only by failing to comply with contemporary standards of reflection. Even if it were so to understand itself as to comply fully with such standards, by acknowledging only completely general criteria of truth and requiring no other qualifications of its students than any study must require, theology could still make good its claim to be different simply by pointing to the question but for asking which it could not exist at all. Nor can there be any doubt whatever whether the difference its question suffices to ground really makes a difference. For while theology certainly is not alone in asking about the meaning and truth of the Christian witness of faith, it certainly is alone in being constituted as such, as the single field-encompassing field of study it is, by just this particular question.

The conventional account notwithstanding, then, the supposed dilemma is merely that, and the usual alternatives are not the only alternatives for dealing with the problem of theology's self-understanding. Because theology can be in full compliance with contemporary standards of reflection even while being really and not merely verbally different from every other field of study, there remains the distinct possibility of a real solution to our problem—a solution that will be adequate at once to the witness of faith itself and to the reflection of our own time.

7

Theology in the University

What is constructive theology, and does it have a place in the liberal arts curriculum of the university?

As I understand it, what presently leads many persons to raise this question is something like the following line of thought: Given both the maturing of religious studies as a discipline and certain recent changes in theology, there would appear to be an opportunity, even a need, for further reflection on the role of constructive theology in the liberal arts curriculum of the university. On the one hand, the study of religion is now well established as a humanistic discipline, as distinct from a confessional or properly theological undertaking. In fact, as the field of religious studies has developed over the last twenty-five years, perfectly reputable historical, philosophical, and social-scientific approaches to the study of religion have now come to predominate over all theological approaches, whose reputation in the modern university is more dubious. On the other hand, an avowedly "revisionist" stream of theological thought emerging from the theological ferment of the 1960s conceives constructive theology as having a source in "common human experience" as well as in "the Christian fact," and hence as being by its very nature a genuinely "university," as distinct from simply a "church," undertaking (Tracy, 1975; 1981). Consequently, these changes in theology as well as the coming of age of religious studies indicate that the time is ripe to ask anew what a properly theological approach to the study of religion might be, and whether such an approach might have a place within the university's liberal arts curriculum.

Assuming that some such reasoning as this is why a number

of persons today are asking the question before us, I propose to speak to it directly and summarily, taking up each of its two parts in turn. In doing so, I shall be depending—particularly in considering the first part—on the more extended discussions in several of the preceding studies.

1

What is constructive theology?

Literally, of course, "theology" means *logos* about *theos*, or thought and speech about God; and this will do as well as anything as an initial answer to our question. But two reflections immediately suggest themselves, the effect of which is first to broaden and then to narrow the literal meaning of the word, and hence the scope of this initial answer.

It becomes evident, first of all, that the same questions to which thought and speech about God function to give an answer may also be given at least verbally different answers by not thinking and speaking about God but about something else instead. To be sure, the word "God" itself can be used so broadly that it means simply the meaning of ultimate reality for us, whatever this meaning may prove to be, or—to speak less existentially and more metaphysically—it may mean simply the structure of ultimate reality in itself, however we may finally conceive this structure. But if "God" is used, as it ordinarily is, in some more restricted, specifically theistic sense, the questions it serves to answer, whether existential or metaphysical, may be answered at least verbally by thinking and speaking about something other than God. Thus one may answer them, for example, by thinking and speaking about Nature or the Absolute, one's Real Self or the whole, Nirvana or the Form of the Good.

Assuming, then, as I do, that the logic of what we think and say is determined by the questions we ask rather than by the answers we give, one is compelled to conclude that the thought and speech that are logically of a piece with theology are considerably broader and more inclusive than ordinary thought and speech about God. They are sufficiently inclusive, in fact, to comprise any and all thinking and speaking about the meaning of ultimate reality for us or its structure in itself, regardless of the terms in which they take place, whether theistic concepts and symbols or not.

But it becomes just as evident, secondly, that although theology is indeed thought and speech about God, or about the ultimate reality about which "God" itself is a way of thinking and speaking, the converse of this proposition does not hold. Not all thought and speech about God are theology, nor are all thought and speech about ultimate reality generally. This is so, at any rate, if one takes account of the strict and proper sense in which "theology" has also come to be used—namely, to refer to either the process or the product of a certain kind of critical reflection. Of course, "theology" is commonly used otherwise than in this narrow sense. In fact, its ordinary meaning is broad enough to cover all thought and speech about God or about ultimate reality, whatever the degree of reflection it happens to involve. And this is certainly understandable, because even the most spontaneous thought and speech involve some degree of reflection and to this extent are a reflective process or product. But there is still an important difference between the thinking and speaking involved in spontaneously experiencing reality and those involved in critically reflecting on the terms in which this experience is already expressed, so as to determine what they really mean and whether the claims they make are really true. Even if the terms used on the second level of reflection are the identical concepts and symbols already used on the first, they nevertheless serve a very different function: not merely to express our experience of reality but also, and primarily, to answer the question about the meaning and truth of the claims in which we spontaneously express it.

If this difference suffices to distinguish critical reflection generally, however, it is also sufficient to distinguish the kind of critical reflection on spontaneous thought and speech about God or about ultimate reality in general that is meant by "theology" in the strict and proper sense. In this sense of the word, theology is not all thinking and speaking about God or the ultimate, but only some—namely, those that are involved in critically reflecting on the meaning of such thinking and speaking and on the credibility of their claims to tell the truth.

So much for the meaning of "theology" as such, without further qualification. As for the qualifier "constructive," I am using it here in contrast with the other qualifier, "descriptive." As questionable an undertaking as theology has widely come to be for many persons in the modern university, few of them would wish to dispute that a descriptive study of religion and, in this sense, a "descriptive theology," may fairly claim a place in the liberal arts curriculum. So far as they are concerned, the real question is whether anything like the same claim can be allowed in the case of what could be called, by contrast, "constructive theology." In other words, if in this usage "descriptive theology" means essentially the same as what contemporary theologians commonly call "historical theology," "constructive theology" is but another way of speaking of what theologians today call "systematic theology."

But this means, then, that what our question asks about is simply theology itself in the sense in which I have already spoken of it, as critical reflection on the meaning and truth of thought and speech about God or ultimate reality, as distinct from such merely descriptive or historical reflection as may be necessary thereto. Of course, as theology has developed as a field of study, it has become ever clearer that historical reflection is indeed necessary to it; and for this reason, such reflection has now come to be generally regarded as itself an integral theological discipline. But, significantly, the convention is also widely observed of distinguishing such historical reflection by some such qualifier as "descriptive" or "historical," while correspondingly qualifying theology itself as "constructive" or "systematic." The significance of this convention is the logical difference to which it points. Just as historical reflection in general is properly concerned to determine the truth about the past, especially the human past, so any reflection that could be appropriately called "historical theology" would be properly concerned to determine the truth about what human beings in the past have thought and said about God or about ultimate reality generally. But to determine the truth about what has been thought and said about God or the ultimate is not to determine whether what has been thought and said about God or the ultimate is the truth; and it is only this second, logically different task that is the proper task of theology itself, or of what is called, in distinction from historical theology, "systematic theology."

I may note, in passing, the bearing of this distinction on the present argument. In answering our question as I am proceeding to do, I am obviously assuming that those who are now asking it are asking, not for a *historical* theological determination of what constructive theology has been thought and said to be, but, rather, for a *systematic* theological determination of what constructive theology really and truly is. Such an assumption seems to me justified if one further assumes, as I do, that the question being asked admits of some kind of theological answer. If what theology itself really and truly is is any kind of theological question at all, it is clearly a systematic, not a historical, theological question.

There remains a further critical step in answering the first part of our question, and to take it requires that we recognize the unique function of religion as a form of human culture.

Constructive theology, I have said, is critical reflection on the meaning and truth of thought and speech about God or about the meaning or structure of ultimate reality generally. But an essential property of ultimate reality, as of any referent of "God" so understood as to be a fit concept and symbol thereof, is ubiquity or omnipresence. This means, among other things, that the ultimate reality to which "God" rightly refers is and must be present in all of our spontaneous experience, so that, in whatever we think and say about anything at all, we are and must be thinking and speaking about just this ultimate reality, even if only implicitly. Consequently, not only religion, but every other form of human culture, necessarily involves at least an implicit reference to God or the ultimate, and hence belongs to the data of theological reflection, in the sense of the thinking and speaking whose meaning and truth theology exists to determine.

Even so, religion is unique because it is the only primary form of culture in which this necessary reference to God or the ultimate also becomes explicit, in concepts and symbols whose direct referent is God, or the ultimate reality that "God" itself functions to conceive and symbolize. Thus if all forms of culture, and hence all thinking and speaking, are data of theological reflection, its privileged data for determining the meaning of what is thought and said about the ultimate are the thought and speech distinctive of religion.

Furthermore, it is characteristic of religion generically, and

hence of every specific religion, to claim tacitly or openly to bear
the decisive revelation of the God, or the decisive re-presentation
of the ultimate reality, that is ubiquitous or omnipresent in all
our spontaneous experience and more or less truthfully explicated in every other specific religion. In other words, the decisive
authority that each religion claims for its own thinking and
speaking over against all other specific religions derives from its
claim to make fully explicit just that truth about God or the ultimate that is and must be told at least implicitly by all that we
think or say as well as explicitly told by any religion precisely
insofar as it is true.

Because, however, there is such a thing as religion, and,
therefore, specific religions each claiming just such a decisive
authority, there is evidently more than one thing that could be
called "constructive theology." There is the possibility, to be exact, of two quite distinct, even if closely related, types of critical
reflection, both of which qualify as constructive theology in the
sense previously clarified.

There is, first of all, the type of theological reflection constituted by human existence as such. Insofar as human beings have
been in any way religious or have so much as thought and spoken about anything at all, they have at least implicitly thought
and spoken about God or the ultimate, and have thereby provided data for inquiring critically as to the meaning and truth of
such thinking and speaking. Moreover, any human being, simply by virtue of the capacity for reflection that makes us human,
would have the ability, if not the willingness, to engage in just
such critical inquiry. Because this type of theological reflection
thus seems possible for any human being simply as such, and
because it also appears to be necessary, finally, to determine the
truth of any specific religion whatever, I find it fitting to distinguish it as *"philosophical* theology." Tradition indicates that one
might also speak of it as "natural theology," were not the presupposed distinction between "natural" and "revealed" (or "supernatural") for various reasons questionable.

Secondly, then, there is the type of theological reflection for
whose constitution human existence simply as such is insufficient. Also necessary for this type of constructive theology is the
claim of some specific religion or other to decisive authority, and
hence the claim to make the truth about God or the ultimate

fully explicit. In other words, if the thought and speech distinctive of religions generally are the privileged data of both types of constructive theology, this second type is distinguished from the first by having, as it were, twice-privileged data in what is thought and said by some one specific religion in advancing its claim to decisive authority and truth.

Thus when "theology" is used to speak of this second type of critical reflection, it has both a generic and a specific meaning. In its generic meaning, which corresponds to the generic sense of "religion," it designates the critical reflection constituted by the question as to the meaning and truth of what is thought and said by a religion, and hence by one or the other of the specific religions as which religion alone exists. But just as religion exists only as specific religions, so theology of this second type exists only as specific theologies cognate with the specific religions on which they are the critical reflection. And so when "theology" is used to speak of this second type of reflection, it also has a specific meaning that can be fully explicated only by some such phrase, say, as "*Christian* theology." This phrase is appropriately used to distinguish the specific theology cognate with the Christian religion, in the sense of the critical reflection constituted by asking about the meaning and truth of specifically Christian thinking and speaking about God as ultimate reality. In more or less the same sense, one might also properly speak of "Jewish theology" or "Buddhist theology" or even, possibly, "Communist theology." Depending on how narrowly or broadly one defines the term "religion," one may reasonably hold that not only Judaism but also Buddhism and even Communism are each a specific religion, of which there may well be a cognate specific theology constituted by the question as to the meaning and truth of this religion's distinctive claims.

Of course, even for Christian theology in this sense, the thought and speech distinctive of the Christian religion are privileged data only with respect to the *meaning* of what is thought and said, not with respect to its truth. In the nature of the case, there cannot be any privileged data with respect to truth, assuming that the truth-claim in question is a universal claim. Thus while philosophical theology has every reason to look to religious thinking and speaking generally to determine what is meant by "God" or by any other concept or symbol of ultimate reality, the only way it can determine what is true in such thinking and speaking is by taking into account all that human beings think and say, secular as well as religious. Similarly, Christian theology has not only the right but also the responsibility to look to specifically Christian thinking and speaking and to what they in turn specify as normative or canonical to determine what the Christian religion means by its claims concerning God. And yet if Christian theology is to determine not only the meaning of Christian claims but also their truth, it is bound by the very logic of the claims themselves to take account of the same strictly universal range of data that philosophical theology has to take into account in making the same determination. For this reason, one must say that philosophical reflection is as necessary, finally, to determine the truth of the Christian religion as it is to determine the truth of any other religion.

Even so, Christian theology, like Jewish theology or Buddhist theology or the theology of any other specific religion, remains distinct from the philosophical theology on which it necessarily depends. Not only would Christian theology not be so much as possible but for the prior existence of the Christian religion on which it is the critical reflection, but, even in taking account of all that human beings think and say, secular as well as religious, it does so only in pursuit of its own constitutive task of determining the meaning and truth of specifically Christian thinking and speaking about God.

2

Does constructive theology have a place in the liberal arts curriculum of the university?

The conclusion we are entitled to draw by all that has been said to this point is that "constructive theology" is a systematically ambiguous phrase, in that its meaning may vary systematically from one context to another, depending on whether we use it to designate one or the other of two distinct types of critical reflection: either the type I call "philosophical theology" or the type represented by what I understand by "Christian theology." Although it has seemed important to me to establish that Christian theology, properly so-called, is but one specific example of a type of theological reflection of which there are, or may be, any number of other examples—as many, indeed, as there are specific religions—it seems clear enough from the line of thinking that leads persons today to ask our question that it is with specifically Christian theology that they are above all concerned. And yet even if this is sufficient reason to focus our discussion henceforth on the place of constructive *Christian* theology, as distinct from the constructive theology of any other specific religion, there remains the distinction between all theologies of this second type, Christian or otherwise, and constructive *philosophical* theology. Accordingly, the second part of our question is really two different questions which call for two different answers— the one having to do with the place of constructive philosophical theology in the liberal arts curriculum, the other having to do with the place, if any, of constructive Christian theology in the same curriculum.

So far as the first question is concerned, the answer can be stated quite simply. Philosophical theology not only does but must have a place in the liberal arts curriculum, provided that religious studies have such a place and that by "religious studies" is meant a single field-encompassing field of study, constituted by a single question for reflection, rather than simply many studies of religion, constituted by the multiple questions of other fields of study. Naturally, one does not have to understand religious studies as a single "field" in the strict sense of the word. But if one does so understand them, one may reasonably be expected to specify the question that constitutes them a single field; and in my own experience and reflection, there is but one proposal for doing this that is at all convincing. This is a proposal to the effect that the question constituting religious studies a single, albeit complex, field of study is the question as to the meaning and truth of religion as the primary way in which human beings make fully explicit the truth about ultimate reality disclosed by their spontaneous experience. If one keeps in mind, then, that the thinking and speaking about ultimate reality that become fully explicit in religion can be true only insofar as they are also at least implicitly attested by all the other forms of culture, obviously, the only way any religion can be studied so as to determine its meaning and truth is in the larger context of all that human beings have thought and said, secular as well as religious. But this means, of course, that the constitutive question of religious studies as a single field necessarily entails asking the distinctive question of philosophical theology. And this is so even if asking exactly the same philosophical theological question is also a constituent part of the other field of philosophy, constituted by its constitutive question as well.

There is no doubt in my mind, then, that constructive *philosophical* theology does indeed have a place in the liberal arts curriculum if religious studies can be said to have such a place. For either "religious studies" designates a proper field of study constituted by the question as to the meaning and truth of religion, and hence by the philosophical theological question as to the meaning and truth of all thinking and speaking about God or the ultimate, or else it is simply a loose way of speaking of what would be less misleadingly called "studies of religion," seeing that they are merely the several studies of religion already constituted by the constitutive questions of other fields of study, such as philosophy, history, and the social sciences.

The answer to the second question, however, cannot be stated quite so simply, at least if one assumes, as I do, that by "liberal arts curriculum" is meant the curriculum of a university that may not be explicitly Christian. It seems reasonable to hold that, if there can be such a thing as an explicitly Christian university at all—and only few, I assume, would wish to deny this—constructive Christian theology does indeed have a place in its liberal arts curriculum. This is a reasonable position, at any rate, if Christian theology is understood, as I have proposed here, as critical reflection on the Christian religion so as to determine its meaning and truth. On this understanding, Christian theology has two chief defining characteristics: it is constituted as a process of reflection simply by the question as to the meaning and truth of what Christians think and say about God; and it cannot fully answer this question, because it cannot determine the truth of their thinking and speaking, except by taking account of all that human beings have thought and said about the ultimate, secular and religious alike. But this means, then, that Christian theology's standards of reflection are no different in principle from those of religious studies or of any other field of study whose place in the liberal arts curriculum is beyond question.

Specifically, Christian theology so understood requires neither special qualifications of its students in the way of prior adherence to the Christian religion, nor special criteria for its claims in the way of criteria of truth sufficiently based only in specifically Christian experience. On the contrary, all that it asks of its students is that they be able and willing to ask the universally human questions about the meaning and structure of ultimate reality, to which all Christian thinking and speaking in one way or another give answers; and all that it demands by way of criteria for its claims are criteria already sufficiently based simply in universally human experience, and hence one and the same with the criteria required to determine the truth of any other claim about God or the ultimate. But if Christian theology's standards of reflection are in both respects perfectly reputable, and thus entitle it to claim a place in the liberal arts curriculum as secure as that of any other field of study, its being, nevertheless, specifically *Christian* theology, whose constitutive task is to determine the meaning and truth of the specifically Christian religion, is evidently entirely fitting in the curriculum of the explicitly *Christian* university.

This is not so, however, where the curriculum in question is that of a university that is not explicitly Christian. Nor is this judgment in any way weakened in force because Christian theology is understood in the (not "revisionist," but, as I prefer to say) revisionary way I have proposed in this study. If those who would deny Christian theology a place in the liberal arts curriculum because it must require special qualifications of its students or special criteria for its claims have failed to reckon with this revisionary understanding, the same is true of those who would affirm such a place for it simply because its standards of reflection are the same in principle as those of any other field of study. Even if Christian theology's standards of reflection are, indeed, the same in principle as those of any other field of study, the fact remains that it is a unique field of study, incomparable with every other. It would not even be possible except for the prior existence of the Christian religion, and it certainly would not be necessary were not critical reflection on this religion a task incumbent upon anyone who either professes it or else is faced with making a responsible decision about its specific claim to decisive authority and truth. As a matter of fact, Christian theology as such, as distinct from philosophical theological reflection on the Christian religion, is strictly necessary solely for

Christians, who have the responsibility of bearing witness to their faith and who, for the sake of this responsibility, must critically reflect on the meaning and truth of its distinctive claims. For once Christian thinking and speaking about God exist, what such thinking and speaking mean and whether or not they are true must already be a question for philosophical theology, rightly understood. Consequently, there is no need for Christian theology as such in order to ask and answer this question, and if Christian theology has any place in the liberal arts curriculum at all, some other justification must be given for it.

One might suppose in this connection that, because the Christian religion has been formative of the whole of the specifically Western cultural heritage, there is reason enough for any Western university, even one that is not explicitly Christian, to include Christian theology in its liberal arts curriculum. But again, what could Christian theology serve to do in any such curriculum that could not already be done by philosophical theology? Assuming only that it would take account, as it certainly should, of the specificially Christian religion, one could confidently leave this task, too, to philosophical theology, whether as constituted by the constitutive question of religious studies or as a constituent part of the field of philosophy.

My answer to the second question, therefore, is that constructive *Christian* theology as such does not necessarily have any place in the liberal arts curriculum of the university. As rightly as it may claim such a place in the curriculum of the explicitly Christian university, it seems quite out of place in the curriculum of any university that is not explicitly Christian. The reason for this, to repeat, is not that the standards of reflection of Christian theology must be regarded as in some respect dubious as compared with those of other fields of study. The reason, rather, is that even though its standards of reflection can very well be regarded as in all respects perfectly reputable, it necessarily presupposes the specifically Christian religion, which cannot be thus presupposed as a necessary condition of the possibility of any but an explicitly Christian university. In this respect, at least, no Christian theology worthy of the name can legitimately claim a place in the curriculum of the university that is not explicitly Christian. This must be said, at any rate, provided that this curriculum includes, either in religious studies or in philosophy, the properly philosophical theological question as to the meaning and truth of all thinking and speaking about the ultimate, and thus of specifically Christian thought and speech about God as well.

8

The Concept of a Theology of Liberation: Must Christian Theology Today Be So Conceived?

1

The fundamental issue with which this study is concerned is how Christian theology itself ought now to be conceived. Consequently, in considering the concept of a theology of liberation, I want to ask whether Christian theology can be adequately conceived only as just such a theology. A claim to this effect I understand to be the main methodological challenge of the several liberation theologies. But my question is whether or to what extent this typical claim is sound and, if or insofar as it is sound, what kinds of reasons may be given to support it.

Obviously, the first thing to do is to try to clarify just what is to be understood by the term, "a theology of liberation." Granted that it is properly used to designate only a certain concept or ideal type of Christian theology, how exactly is this type to be constructed? For purposes of this discussion, I propose to construct it simply from some methodological reflections of Gustavo Gutiérrez, whose contribution at this point I regard as outstanding. The disadvantages of such a procedure are clear. But provided we keep in mind that it is only insofar as particular theologies conform to the type to be thus constructed that they fall subject to the judgments I shall make about them, there should not be any serious difficulty. At any rate, the clear advantage of the procedure is that it allows us to confront the challenge of liberation theology concretely, in at least one of the forms in which it is actually being made.

According to Gutiérrez, Christian theology today, given the present historical situation, is adequately conceived only as "critical reflection on historical praxis, flowing out of that praxis and a confrontation with the word of the Lord that is accepted and lived by faith" (1979: 22; cf. 1976: 40). I select this formulation because it seems to me both more explicit and more balanced than other formulations where Gutiérrez speaks of theology simply as "reflection in and on faith as a liberating praxis" (1976: 40–41). The difficulty with this second kind of formulation is that, if it is taken simply by itself, out of its proper context, it may lead to either or both of two misunderstandings of Gutiérrez's intention.

On the one hand, it may obscure the distinction he expressly makes between *"historical* praxis" and *"liberating* praxis." The first is the activity essential to human existence as such, by which men and women continually transform the natural and social conditions of their lives, thereby creating themselves and one another, while the second is what such historical praxis becomes or should become insofar as, under conditions of injustice—social, economic, cultural, or racial—human beings act out of solidarity with the oppressed so as to transform the structures oppressing them (30). There is no question, of course, that Gutiérrez understands the conditions under which we live today to be so profoundly unjust that our historical praxis certainly ought to assume the form of just such a liberating praxis, even to the point of immersing us in "the political process of revolution" (1979: 24). Even so, to ignore the fact that the connection here is contingent is, in effect, to confuse things that he himself is at some pains clearly to distinguish.

On the other hand, his meaning is even more seriously misunderstood if faith is taken to be nothing other than human praxis, whether generally historical or specifically liberating. As insistent as he is that faith is much more than a theoretical matter of believing certain things *about* God, because it is the eminently practical matter of believing *in* God, he is also emphatic that this practical faith that works through love is "the acceptance of the Father's love and a response to it" (20). In other words, the human praxis of faith has its necessary ground in a divine action prior to it and hence is lived, as Gutiérrez puts it, as "a confrontation with the word of the Lord."

In this understanding, then, the faith on which theology critically reflects is not merely singly but doubly determined: on the one side, by the historical praxis which, in our situation today, must be the praxis of liberation; and on the other side, by "the mystery of divine adoption and brotherhood that lay hidden from all eternity and was eventually revealed in Jesus Christ," whose gospel "reveals us to be children of our heavenly Father and brothers and sisters of others" (26).

As critical reflection on faith thus doubly determined, theology exhibits the same double determination, albeit as "a second act" of reflection relative to the first act of faith itself (1976: 42). The reason for this is that theology is reflection *in* faith as well as *on* it and is entirely oriented to the communication of faith through the proclamation of the gospel (40–41, 16). As a matter of fact, Gutiérrez understands theology and faith to be so closely related that he can say not only that "liberation theology comes only after involvement" but also that it is "a necessary precondition if their work is to be concrete and scientific" that "theologians themselves must be persons involved in the process of liberation" (42; 1979: 33, n. 9).

Here, again, the one-sidedness of Gutiérrez's formulations may only too easily mislead as to what he really means to say. Given his insistence that theology is a process of understanding faith that is based in a prior option for the oppressed and a commitment to their liberation, it may well appear that theology consists simply in what he speaks of as "a re-reading of the gospel message from within the context of liberation praxis" (1979: 25). But this, I am confident, would be a serious misunderstanding of Gutiérrez's meaning. If he argues that theological reflection "is rooted in a commitment to create a just and communal society," he also maintains that such reflection "in turn should help to make this commitment more radical and complete" (22). Nor can there be any doubt about what he means by this. Just as he understands that "the root of social injustice is sin, which ruptures our friendship with God and our brotherhood with other human beings," so he understands "Christ's liberation" to be "a radical liberation, which necessarily includes liberation of a political nature," although it is "not restricted to political liberation" (20–21, 23). In short, what Gutiérrez means by theology's making the commitment to social justice more radical and complete—or, as he can also say, "more self-critical"— is precisely its "framing the political commitment to liberation within the context of Christ's gratuitous gift of total liberation" (23). Thus, speaking of the two forms of liberation that remain distinct even though integrally related, he can defend himself and his fellow liberation theologians by protesting that "we are not engaging in facile but denigratory equations, distortions, or simplistic forms of reductionism; instead we are shedding light on both sides and showing how their exigencies complement and fructify one another" (23). In the same vein, he voices the confidence that "the future lies with a kind of faith and ecclesial communion that is not afraid of advances in human thinking and social praxis, that is open to questioning by them and ready to challenge them in turn, that is willing to be enriched but is not uncritical, that knows its own conditioning factors but also its own proper exigencies" (19).

Thus as Gutiérrez presents it, a liberation theology is like most other types of Christian theology, past and present, in being a critical reflection on Christian faith oriented to the communication of faith through the proclamation of the gospel. What distinguishes it from other types of theology is the prior commitment of faith on which it is the reflection, which is a commitment not only to the gospel as attested by scripture and tradition but also to fellow human beings insofar as, being victims of structural injustice, they are somehow moved by the question of freedom from their oppression. As such, therefore, a theology of liberation involves a re-reading of the gospel from within the context of the liberating praxis that grows out of this commitment and is directed toward responding to the question of the oppressed by transforming existing conditions.

Negatively, this re-reading takes the form of what I shall call (although, so far as I know, Gutiérrez does not) a deideologizing of the gospel, in that it involves so reinterpreting the gospel's meaning as to disengage it from all interpretations whereby in one way or another it has been made to sanction existing injustice and oppression. Positively, this re-reading of the gospel takes the form of its political, even revolutionary, interpretation, in the sense that the gospel's gift and demand of a faith that works through love is interpreted as necessarily including a praxis of liberation that in our situation today is not only political but must even be subversive of the standing order of injustice. At the same time, a theology of liberation, as Gutiérrez understands it, also involves something like a reverse re-reading of the whole political and revolutionary process to which faith as a liberating praxis is necessarily committed. This it involves because, being Christian theology in the full and proper sense of the words, it cannot but place the commitment to political liberation in the larger and deeper context of God's gift and demand of total liberation in Christ, thereby rendering the whole praxis of liberation more radical and complete as well as more self-critical.

If we assume now that something like this is what a theology of liberation typically involves, we may say that any such theology must be conceived to have two defining characteristics. Its first and formal defining characteristic is its understanding of the critical reflection in which it itself consists as one particular expression of the faith on which it reflects. More exactly, it understands theological reflection to be not only contingently but necessarily an expression of faith, in that such reflection is not really possible at all unless it arises out of the theologian's own prior commitment as a Christian believer. The second and, by contrast, material defining characteristic of a liberation theology is its understanding of the faith on which it as theology reflects, and of which it itself is necessarily an expression. Specifically, it understands Christian faith to be essentially a loving praxis that, under existing conditions of structural injustice, must necessarily become a commitment to the political, even revolutionary, liberation of the oppressed. Thus if the first defining characteristic of a theology of liberation allows one to conceive of theological reflection as being of direct service to the proclamation of the gospel, and hence to the praxis of liberation, its second defining characteristic requires one to conceive of theology as necessarily including a deideologizing of the gospel together with its political, indeed, revolutionary interpretation.

2

Having constructed the concept or ideal type that the term "a theology of liberation" is properly used to designate, I turn to the claim, also typical of theologies of liberation, that any adequate Christian theology today must be conceived in conformity with just this concept or type. Clearly, the question of whether this claim is sound cannot be given a reasoned answer except from some methodological standpoint. Consequently, the next thing I have to do is to try to provoke reflection on the concept of Christian theology by offering a summary characterization of my own.

As I conceive it, Christian theology is formally characterized as either the process or the product of a certain kind of critical reflection. As a *process* of reflection, it is the kind constituted as such by the twofold question as to the meaning and truth of the Christian witness of faith. Therefore, insofar as it involves any prior commitment, it is committed simply to understanding the meaning of the Christian witness and to assessing its truth, and, therefore, to any and all human beings insofar as, being human, they are somehow moved by the question of the ultimate meaning of their existence to which this witness presents itself as the answer. As a *product* of this kind of reflection, by contrast, theology is constituted as such, not by a question, but by an answer—specifically, by a reasoned answer to its question of the meaning of the Christian witness and, on this basis, a positive answer to its question of the truth of this witness that is likewise a reasoned answer. Thus, insofar as theology as a product of reflection involves any prior commitment, it is a commitment not only to the truth of the Christian witness, given some understanding of its meaning, but also to giving reasons for the claim that this witness is true. As such, therefore, it is once again a commitment to any and all human beings insofar as, being human, they not only ask about the ultimate meaning of their existence but are also bound to seek only the truth in doing so.

On this conception, there are evidently two kinds of reasons that can and must be given for any theological claim, including such methodological claims as theology must make about itself. On the one hand, there is the kind of reasons required by any reasoned answer to its question concerning the meaning of the Christian witness. Insofar as a theological claim is sound, the first thing to be said about it is that it is *appropriate*, in the sense of being congruent in meaning with the witness of faith itself. Clearly, whether a claim is thus congruent can be determined only by first determining the real meaning of the witness of faith, and such reasons as one may give for its congruence all depend on this prior determination. In the final analysis, the real meaning of the Christian witness is the real meaning of the *canonical* Christian witness, and just what is to be understood as constituting the Christian canon has been and remains controversial in theology. But on the principle, which I believe to be sound, that the criterion of canonicity is and must be apostolicity, the real meaning of the Christian witness is the meaning to be discerned in the witness of the apostles as their witness can and must be determined by the best historical methods and knowledge available in the situation. Accordingly, in my view, the first kind of reasons that can and must be given for a theological claim are reasons purporting to establish its appropriateness to the apostolic witness of faith attested by scripture and tradition.

On the other hand, there is the second kind which comprises the reasons required by any reasoned answer to theology's question about the truth of the Christian witness. If a theological claim is sound, it is so not only because it is appropriate in the sense just explained, but also because it is *credible*, in the sense that it is congruent with the truth disclosed at least implicitly in human existence as such. Of course, any effort to determine this congruence, and to give reasons for it of the kind required, at once becomes involved in even greater controversy. Nothing is more controversial among human beings than just what are to count as the standards or criteria for determining the credibility of their various claims. Even so, if one may say, as I would, that the ultimate criteria for the truth of any claim can only be our common human experience and reason, however hard their verdict may be to determine, then the second kind of reasons that can and must be given for a theological claim are reasons purporting to establish its credibility in terms of what all of us somehow experience and understand, if only implicitly.

Insofar as theology involves the same human understanding involved in any other kind of critical reflection, it is exactly like everything else human in being thoroughly conditioned both socially and culturally. This means, among other things, that theological reflection always and of necessity takes place in some particular historical situation, in terms of its agenda of problems and of its resources for clarifying and solving them. Consequently, while the demand remains constant that any sound theological claim must be supported by reasons purporting to establish both its appropriateness and its credibility, exactly what this demand requires is also always variable in that it is a function of different historical situations. Because this is so, reasons that would be sufficient to establish the soundness of a claim in one situation may very well not be sufficient to do so in another.

As for the reasons that I should give in our situation today for the soundness of this concept of theology, they, too, as I have indicated, must be the same two kinds of reasons, purporting to show that it is both credible and appropriate. So far as its credibility is concerned, suffice it to say that it seems to be in full compliance with standards of critical reflection that are currently widely accepted. Thus, unlike most other concepts of theology, it requires the theologian neither to make the prior commitment of Christian faith nor to appeal at some point to special criteria of truth other than those given generally in our common human experience and reason. But if this much, at least, can be said for its credibility, there seem good reasons to think that it is also appropriate. This is so, at any rate, if the exegetical argument is sound that in the apostolic witness attested by scripture it is typically assumed that the claims of the Christian witness are true, in the final analysis, for the very same reason that any other claim is true—namely, because they express explicitly and fully what anyone to whom they are addressed at least implicitly understands, and, but for willful suppression of the truth, would also be led to affirm by his or her own experience and reason.

Certainly, this is the assumption when the Johannine Jesus is represented as saying, "My teaching is not mine, but his who sent me; if any man's will is to do his will, he shall know whether the teaching is from God, or whether I am speaking on my own authority" (Jn. 7:16–17); or again, when Paul represents the method of his own witness of faith by saying that "by the open statement of the truth we would commend ourselves to every man's conscience in the sight of God. And even if our gospel is veiled, it is veiled only to those who are perishing" (2 Cor. 4:2–3).

But if the concept of Christian theology for which I should thus argue can be established as both credible and appropriate, there is clearly one important respect in which the answer to the question before us must be negative: Christian theology today must *not* be conceived as a theology of liberation.

I refer, of course, to what I distinguished earlier as the formal defining characteristic of the typical liberation theology. Whereas on the concept I have just summarized, Christian theology is already constituted as a process of critical reflection by asking the twofold question as to the meaning and truth of the Christian witness, and is constituted as a product of such reflection by giving a reasoned answer to this question asserting the truth of the Christian witness, on the concept typical of a theology of liberation, the prior commitment involved in thus asking or answering this reflective question is insufficient to constitute Christian theology as such. Also necessary is the prior commitment involved in the actual existence of Christian faith as a historical praxis of love, which, in our situation today, means both an acceptance of God's prevenient love for us and a praxis of liberating our oppressed brothers and sisters by political activity directed toward transforming the conditions oppressing them. Unless and until this commitment of faith is made, liberation theologians contend, there cannot be the kind of critical reflection that is properly Christian theology, whatever other conditions may also be necessary in order for it to take place.

From my own methodological standpoint, however, such plausibility as this contention may claim turns upon mistaking a contingent connection for a necessary one, thereby confusing two things that should be clearly distinguished—namely, theology as such, as critical reflection on the Christian witness, and theology undertaken as a Christian vocation. Certainly, insofar as a theologian is a Christian believer and has assumed theological responsibility for this very reason, he or she may fairly be held accountable for making the same prior commitment that must be made by any other Christian. But even in this case it is critical to realize that what makes one a theologian, insofar as one is such, is not the commitment of faith one shares as a believing Christian, but only reflectively asking and answering the question as to the meaning and truth of the Christian witness, together with making whatever prior commitment this kind of reflection involves. So far, then, from being a necessary precondition of their work's being concrete and scientific, the involvement of theologians in the process of liberation is really necessary to their being Christians and to their work's being a Christian vocation. On the contrary, what is really a necessary precondition of their theology's being concrete and scientific is that it go beyond merely assuming the truth of their prior commitment as Christians to ask and answer the question of whether the claims implied in this commitment are really true. In fact, unless and until they subject even the constitutive claims of faith itself to the question of truth, their reflection must remain bound so closely to the faith on which it is supposed to reflect that, while it may indeed be a reflection *in* faith, it cannot be a reflection *on* faith, because the only things of which it can really be critical are the expressions of faith in witness.

At stake, in short, is whether Christian theology is to be conceived as critical reflection on witness in the full and proper sense of the words, in which case its service to witness must be indirect only, or whether it is to be regarded as being of direct service to the proclamation of the gospel and the praxis of faith only because it is conceived, in effect, as the mere rationalization of positions already taken. If I am right, the second concept cannot fairly claim to be either appropriate or credible, given the best insights of our present situation, while good reasons can be given to show that the first concept is both appropriate and credible in terms of those same insights. Indeed, I am prepared to argue that it is solely this first concept that can adequately express the legitimate motives of a theology of liberation itself. For this concept alone can do justice both to the deep aspiration of all human beings to know the truth that makes them free and to the Christian witness of faith that claims to re-present this liberating truth.

3

Yet as important as it is to realize what is at stake with respect to this first or formal characteristic of a theology of liberation, we still have to consider its typical claim with respect to its second or material characteristic. Not to recognize this would be to make a double mistake. Not only is the logical connection

between the two characteristics contingent rather than necessary, but the formal characteristic alone by no means suffices to
distinguish liberation theology as a unique ideal type. On the
contrary, it is just this first characteristic that makes it like, rather
than different from, most other types of Christian theology. Almost all Christian theologies, historic as well as contemporary,
have so understood themselves as to be in effect, if not in intention, instances of rationalization rather than critical reflection,
at least when judged by the best current standards of judgment.
Consequently, for both of these reasons, we need to consider
carefully the material characteristic of a liberation theology in its
own right before dismissing its claim to be the only way in which
Christian theology today can be adequately conceived.

What can be said for its claim, then, with respect to its understanding of faith as a liberating praxis? My answer is that
quite a bit can be said for it—enough, in fact, to establish it as
theologically sound.

One reason I speak with some confidence about this is that
a theology of liberation may fairly lay claim to all the reasons
that have already been given in support of such an understanding of faith by those who have argued with Rudolf Bultmann
that Christian theology today must be an existentialist theology.
I do not mean by this that there are no important differences
between an existentialist theology such as Bultmann's and a liberation theology like Gutiérrez's, or that existentialist theologians
have already anticipated the understanding of faith for which
liberation theologians are now contending. But I do mean that
the understanding of faith that both implies and is implied by
an existentialist theology, which proceeds negatively by way of
demythologizing, and positively by way of existentialist interpretation, is an understanding of faith precisely as praxis, as a
way of existing and acting *in* history rather than merely thinking
and believing certain things *about* it or about some other non-
historical realm unrelated to it. To this extent, a liberation theology can legitimately claim the support of an existentialist
theology for the understanding of faith as liberating praxis,
which both implies and is implied by the deideologizing and
political interpretation that are the negative and positive moments, respectively, of its own theological method.

There is a further reason for my confidence that the claim of a liberation theology can be established as sound as regards its understanding of faith. At the very point where this understanding of faith is different from that of an existentialist theology—and, as I believe, quite rightly different—it is possible to develop an argument for it that point for point parallels Bultmann's earlier argument and is at least comparably sound. To give some idea of what I have in mind, I want to indicate briefly a few of the points that such an argument could be made to include.

It will be recalled that Bultmann argues for the necessity of demythologizing by pointing to the conflict between a mythical picture of the world and the world-picture of modern science together with our modern understanding of our own existence. Because the modern elements in this conflict are simply givens in our historical situation, the credibility of the kerygma as a message addressed to us turns on the possibility of critically interpreting the mythology in terms of which it has traditionally been expressed, and in this sense on demythologizing it. The question Bultmann then presses is whether the demythologizing he has thus shown to be necessary is really possible—or in other words, whether a procedure that can alone meet the demand for credibility can also meet the demand for appropriateness. To this question, then, he argues for an affirmative answer, for which at this point in his argument he gives two closely related reasons. The first is that it is the very nature of myth in general that, although its terms and categories are those of our ordinary objectifying thinking, its real intention is to express an understanding of our own existence in the world in relation to its primal source and final end. And the second reason is that the prevailing use of myth in the New Testament in particular is precisely for the sake of thus expressing an understanding of human existence, rather than in any way satisfying an interest in a merely objectifying picture of the world (1984: 1–11).

Now this whole line of argument can be paralleled point for point to support the procedure of deideologizing that, as we have seen, is an essential moment in the method of a theology of liberation. This is certainly so as regards the necessity of such deideologizing, as is clear from arguments developed by liberation theologians themselves. Gutiérrez, for example, argues that, whereas much contemporary theology seeks to respond to the challenge of the *"non-believer,"* who questions our *"religious world*" as Christians, in a continent like Latin America the primary challenge comes to us, rather, from the "*non-person*" who, being excluded from the existing order, questions us about our "*economic, social, political, and cultural world*" (1976: 37). What is clearly necessary, then, if the credibility of the gospel is to be maintained in face of this kind of challenge is to deideologize it, in the sense of so reinterpreting its meaning as to disengage it from the economic, social, political, and cultural world whose injustices it is used to sanction. But if this much of a parallel argument has already been developed, I see no reason why one cannot go on to develop the rest of it. On the contrary, it seems clear to me that, having argued that deideologizing is necessary, one can give two precisely parallel reasons why it is also possible—or, in the terms we have used here, why it is appropriate as well as credible.

Consider, first, what is properly meant by "ideology." In general, it means a more or less comprehensive understanding of human existence, of how to be and to act as a human being, that functions to justify the interests of a particular group or individual by representing these interests as the claims of disinterested justice. Thus, by its very nature, an ideology's actual effect, if not its real intention, is to rationalize particular interests, even though it represents these interests in terms of a justice that is universal. But this means that, insofar as the interests an ideology functions to justify are not in fact just, it itself provides the criterion for critically interpreting them by its own representation of them as just claims. In this way, the deideologizing of the gospel that is clearly necessary if it is to be credible to those who suffer from oppression and injustice can also be said to be possible, in that it is a procedure appropriate to the very nature of ideology itself.

This conclusion can be further supported, then, by considering the prevailing use of ideology in the apostolic witness attested by the writings of the New Testament. I cannot go into the details of what I understand this to involve, but the gist of the matter is effectively set forth by my colleague Victor Furnish in his book *The Moral Teaching of Paul*. Rightly to interpret Paul's teaching on particular moral issues, Furnish argues, one must take pains to avoid two common ways of abstracting his teaching from its actual context: from the social, cultural, and political situation in and for which it was intended; and from the comprehensive theological understanding in which it is grounded and of which it is a necessary part. On the other hand, keeping this context fully in mind permits us to see that the importance of Paul's moral instructions to us, as distinct from those to whom he actually issued them, lies

. . . less in the particular patterns of conduct they promote than in the underlying concerns and commitments they reveal. They show us faith being enacted in love, and love seeking to effect its transforming power in the midst of this present age. . . . In effect, the concrete ethical teaching of Paul requires us to reformulate every question about our life in the world into the question about our common life before God. It requires us to understand that faith is not faith until it is enacted in love. And it requires us to find out what this means concretely, given the realities of our own place and time, and to do it (Furnish: 27, 138).

Assuming, as I do, that Furnish's conclusions about Paul can be generalized to apply to the way ideology tends to be used throughout the New Testament, I cannot but see this use as yet a second reason why the deideologizing called for by a theology of liberation is appropriate as well as credible.

But I should not want to give the impression that I suppose it is on making particular points similar to these that the argument for understanding Christian faith as a praxis of liberation depends. Whatever weight such points may finally carry, I take the solid foundations of this argument to lie elsewhere and to be all the more secure because they may claim the full support, by clear implication, at least, of an existentialist theology. These foundations, as I see them, are two, and, as might be expected, they have to do respectively with the appropriateness and the credibility of this understanding of faith.

The first foundation is that the faith expressed and implied by the apostolic witness attested by scripture is precisely a faith that, as Paul puts it, works by love. Given the support for this claim throughout the Christian tradition, especially in the theology of the Reformers and, as we have seen, in the existentialist theology of our own time, few theological claims could be more securely established. Moreover, as we have just noted in the case of Paul, the praxis of love apart from which faith is not faith is understood to be by its very nature unbounded in that it governs the full scope of human responsibility and is addressed to the full range of human need. This is why it is always seeking to effect its transforming power in the present world, finding expression in concrete acts of service directed toward meeting any and all human needs. To this extent, the faith attested by the New Testament may be said to be a praxis of love that both seeks justice and finds expression in it.

But to infer simply from this that it is also what a theology of liberation means by liberating praxis is clearly unwarranted. For as we saw earlier, what is properly meant by *"liberating praxis"* is a special form of something more general called *"historical* praxis," which means the essential human activity whereby men and women play their proper role as the active subjects of history, and not merely its passive objects, by continually transforming the conditions of their lives, both natural and social. While some mode of this activity is of the essence of human existence, being the very thing that distinguishes us as human, explicit consciousness of ourselves as thus historical is itself a product of our continuing history. As a matter of fact, it is a relatively recent product, in that it has only gradually emerged in the course of the revolutionary transformations, scientific and technological as well as political, that have created the modern world. Just such explicit consciousness, however, is evidently involved in the special form of historical praxis that is properly liberating; for being the form of praxis that is directed toward transforming the conditions of injustice and oppression, liberating praxis is borne by the consciousness that we ourselves are the agents of history who bear full responsibility for the social and cultural structures of our life together. Consequently, it is plainly anachronistic and, for this reason, unwarranted to infer that the praxis of love and justice attested by scripture is in the full and proper sense a liberating praxis.

Once given modern historical consciousness, however, the praxis of love and justice that scripture undoubtedly does attest faith to be can be rightly interpreted only as being or essentially including the praxis of liberation. For as we have seen, what is striking about the praxis of love attested by the New Testament is that it is unlimited in that it is coextensive not only with the full range of human need but also with the full scope of human responsibility. But, of course, the whole effect of historical consciousness must be to extend the scope of our responsibility to include maintaining and transforming the very structures of society and culture. Insofar as we know that even these basic conditions of our existence are neither divinely appointed nor naturally given but historically created by such as ourselves, we must also know that ours is the responsibility for either maintaining them in the forms in which we have received them from our predecessors or else so transforming them that they more nearly realize the justice that could alone justify maintaining them.

There cannot be the slightest question that this double knowledge is one of the givens of our historical situation as modern Western men and women. Just as this situation is determined by the world-picture of modern science and technology, so the understanding of ourselves by which it is also determined includes necessarily a historical consciousness and the enlarged responsibility it carries with it. In fact, it is clear that all of these givens of our situation are so profoundly interdependent that any one of them must be as essential to it as all the others. But this can mean only that the historical consciousness necessary to faith's being rightly interpreted as a liberating praxis is most certainly given and that it is, therefore, entirely proper to speak of its being given as the second firm foundation for the material claim of a theology of liberation. Because we now know of our responsibility for the entire social and cultural order of which we are a part, we also know that the praxis of love can no longer be only or even primarily the task of meeting needs arising within this existing order. Rather, the primary, if not the only, task of a loving praxis is precisely the liberating praxis whereby the existing order itself is so transformed as to include all the others who must still suffer the oppression of being excluded from it.

My conclusion, then, is that the understanding of faith with which a liberation theology typically challenges us is theologically sound. Indeed, if the final defense of an existentialist theology is that it is the contemporary expression with respect to knowledge of the Pauline doctrine that we are justified by faith alone without the works of the law (Bultmann, 1984: 122), it seems to me that the final, and comparably sufficient, defense of a theology of liberation is that it is the contemporary expression with respect to action of the equally Pauline doctrine that the only faith that justifies us is the faith that works by love. In this second important respect, then, my own answer to the question of this study can only be affirmative: Christian theology today *must* be conceived as a theology of liberation.

Works Cited

Baillie, John. *The Idea of Revelation in Recent Thought*. New York: Columbia University Press, 1956.

Barr, James. *The Bible in the Modern World*. New York: Harper & Row, 1973.

Barth, Karl. *Nein! Antwort an Emil Brunner*. Munich: Christian Kaiser Verlag, 1934.

Baum, Gregory. "'The Religions' in Recent Roman Catholic Theology." *Journal of Religious Thought* 26 (1969) 2: 41–56.

Benn, Stanley I. "Authority." In *The Enclyclopedia of Philosophy*, ed. Paul Edwards. New York: Macmillan Publishing Co., 1967: 1: 215–218.

Brunner, Emil. *Natur und Gnade, Zum Gespräch mit Karl Barth*. Zürich: Zwingli Verlag, 1934.

Bultmann, Rudolf. "Offenbarung: IV. Im NT." In *Religion in Geschichte und Gegenwart*, vol. 4, ed. Hermann Gunkel and Leopold Zscharnach. 2d ed. Tübingen: J. C. B. Mohr, 1930: 661–664.

———. *Theologie des Neuen Testaments*. Tübingen: J. C. B. Mohr, 1948–1953.

———. *Das Urchristentum im Rahmen der antiken Religionen*. Zürich: Artemis Verlag, 1949.

———. *Glauben und Verstehen*, vol. 2. Tübingen: J. C. B. Mohr, 1952.

———. *Glauben und Verstehen*, vol. 1. 2d ed. Tübingen: J. C. B. Mohr, 1954.

———. *Glauben und Verstehen*, vol. 4. Tübingen: J. C. B. Mohr, 1965.

———. *New Testament and Mythology and Other Basic Writings*, ed. and trans. Schubert M. Ogden. Philadelphia: Fortress Press, 1984.

Campenhausen, Hans Freiherr von. *Die Entstehung der christlichen Bibel*. Tübingen: J. C. B. Mohr, 1968.

———. "Die Entstehung des Neuen Testaments." In *Das Neue Testament als Kanon, Dokumentation und kritische Analyse zur gegenwärtigen Diskussion*, ed. Ernst Käsemann. Göttingen: Vandenhoeck & Ruprecht, 1970: 109–123.

Coreth, Emerich, S. J. *Metaphysik, Eine methodisch-systematische Grundlegung*. 2d ed. Innsbruck: Tyrolia Verlag, 1964.

Denzinger, Heinrich, ed. *Enchiridion Symbolorum Definitionum et Declarationum de Rebus Fidei et Morum*. 33d ed. Freiburg: Herder Verlag, 1965.

Flew, Antony. *God and Philosophy*. New York: Harcourt, Brace & World, 1966.

Furnish, Victor Paul. *The Moral Teaching of Paul: Selected Issues*. 2d ed. Nashville, TN: Abingdon Press, 1985.

Gager, John G. "The Gospels and Jesus: Some Doubts about Method." *Journal of Religion* 54 (1974): 244–272.

Geertz, Clifford. "Religion as a Cultural System." In *The Religious Situation*, ed. Donald R. Cutler. Boston: Beacon Press, 1968: 639–688.

Gehlen, Arnold. *Der Mensch, Seine Natur und seine Stellung in der Welt*. 8th ed. Frankfurt: Athenaeum Verlag, 1966.

Gutiérrez, Gustavo. "Faith as Freedom: Solidarity with the Alienated and Confidence in the Future." In *Living with Change, Experience, Faith*, ed. Francis A. Eigo. Villanova, PA: Villanova University Press, 1976: 15–54.

―――. "Liberation Praxis and Christian Faith." In *Frontiers of Theology in Latin America*, ed. Rosino Gibellini. Maryknoll, NY: Orbis Books, 1979: 1–33.

Haendler, Otto. *Grundriss der praktischen Theologie*. Berlin: Alfred Töpelmann, 1957.

Harnack, Adolf von. *Die Entstehung der christlichen Theologie und des kirchlichen Dogmas*. Stuttgart: Ehrenfried Klotz Verlag, 1927.

Hartshorne, Charles. *Man's Vision of God and the Logic of Theism*. Chicago: Willett, Clark & Co., 1941.

―――. *Reality as Social Process: Studies in Metaphysics and Religion*. Glencoe, IL: Free Press, 1953.

―――. *The Logic of Perfection and Other Essays in Neoclassical Metaphysics*. La Salle, IL: Open Court Publishing Co., 1962.

―――. *A Natural Theology for Our Time*. La Salle, IL: Open Court Publishing Co., 1967.

Heidegger, Martin. *Phänomenologie und Theologie*. Frankfurt: Vittorio Klostermann, 1970.

Heppe, Heinrich. *Die Dogmatik der evangelisch-reformierten Kirche dargestellt und aus den Quellen belegt*, ed. Ernst Bizer. 2d ed. Neukirchen: Neukirchener Verlag, 1958.

Hudson, W. D. *Ludwig Wittgenstein: The Bearing of His Philosophy upon Religious Belief*. Richmond, VA: John Knox Press, 1968.

Kähler, Martin. *Der sogennante historische Jesus und der geschichtliche, biblische Christus*, ed. Ernst Wolf. 2d ed. Munich: Christian Kaiser Verlag, 1953.

Kierkegaard, Søren. *Philosophical Fragments: Or a Fragment of Philosophy*, trans. David F. Swenson and Howard V. Hong. 2d ed. Princeton, NJ: Princeton University Press, 1962.

Lonergan, Bernard J. F., S. J. *Method in Theology*. New York: Herder & Herder, 1972.

Luther, Martin. *D. Martin Luthers Werke, Kritische Gesamtausgabe*. Weimar: Hermann Böhlau, 1883–.

Marxsen, Willi. *Anfangsprobleme der Christologie*. Gütersloh: Gütersloher Verlagshaus Gerd Mohn, 1960.

―――. *Das Neue Testament als Buch der Kirche*. Gütersloh: Gütersloher Verlagshaus Gerd Mohn, 1968a.

―――. *Introduction to the New Testament: An Approach to Its Problems*, trans. Geoffrey Buswell. Philadelphia: Fortress Press, 1968b.

―――. *Der Exeget als Theologe, Vorträge zum Neuen Testament*. 2d ed. Gütersloh: Gütersloher Verlagshaus Gerd Mohn, 1969.

Niebuhr, H. Richard. *Radical Monotheism and Western Culture*. New York: Harper & Brothers, 1960.

Niebuhr, Reinhold. *The Nature and Destiny of Man: A Christian Interpretation*. New York: Charles Scribner's Sons, 1941–1943.

Ogden, Schubert M., ed. *Existence and Faith: Shorter Writings of Rudolf Bultmann*. New York: Meridian Books, 1960.

Ott, Heinrich. "Was ist systematische Theologie?" *Zeitschrift für Theologie und Kirche*, Beiheft 2 (1961): 19–46.

Otto, Gert. *Einführung in die praktische Theologie, Ein Arbeitsbuch*. Stuttgart: W. Kohlhammer Verlag, 1976.

Otto, Gert, ed. *Praktisch Theologisches Handbuch*. 2d ed. Hamburg: Furche-Verlag, 1975.

Packer, J. I. *"Fundamentalism" and the Word of God: Some Evangelical Principles*. Grand Rapids, MI: William B. Eerdmans Publishing Co., 1958.

Palmer, C. D. F. "Zur praktischen Theologie." *Jahrbücher für deutsche Theologie* 1 (1856): 317–361.

Passmore, John. *Philosophical Reasoning*. London: Gerald Duckworth & Co., 1961.

Patterson, Ronald P. *et al.*, eds. *The Book of Discipline of the United Methodist Church*. Nashville, TN: United Methodist Publishing House, 1984.

Phillips, D. Z. *Faith and Philosophical Enquiry*. New York: Schocken Books, 1971.

Pieper, Franz. *Christliche Dogmatik*. St. Louis, MO: Concordia Publishing House, 1924.

Plessner, Helmuth. *Die Stufen des Organischen und der Mensch*. 2d ed. Berlin: Walter de Gruyter & Co., 1965.

Pregeant, William Russell. *The Meaning of Matthew's Christology: A Hermeneutical Investigation in Conversation with the Theology of Schubert M. Ogden*. Ann Arbor, MI: University Microfilms, 1971.

Rahner, Karl, S. J., and Ratzinger, Joseph, S. J. *Offenbarung und Überlieferung*. Freiburg: Herder Verlag, 1965.

Ritschl, Dietrich. "A Plea for the Maxim: Scripture and Tradition." *Interpretation* 25 (1971): 113–128.

Rössler, Dietrich. "Prolegomena zur praktischen Theologie, Das Vermächtnis Christian Palmers." *Zeitschrift für Theologie und Kirche* 64 (1967): 357–371.

Rubinoff, Lionel, ed. *Faith and Reason: Essays in the Philosophy of Religion by R. G. Collingwood*. Chicago: Quadrangle Books, 1968.

Santayana, George. *Scepticism and Animal Faith: Introduction to a System of Philosophy*. New York: Charles Scribner's Sons, 1923.

Schleiermacher, Friedrich. *Kurze Darstellung des theologischen Studiums zum Behuf einleitender Vorlesungen*, ed. Heinrich Scholz. 3d ed. Leipzig: A. Deichert, 1910.

————. *Der christliche Glaube nach den Grundsätzen der evangelischen Kirche im Zusammenhang dargestellt*, ed. Martin Redeker. 7th ed. Berlin: Walter de Gruyter & Co., 1960.

Schmid, Heinrich. *Die Dogmatik der evangelisch-lutherischen Kirche dargestellt und aus den Quellen belegt*, ed. Horst Georg Pöhlmann. 10th ed. Gütersloh: Gütersloher Verlagshaus Gerd Mohn, 1983.

Strecker, Georg. "Die historische und theologische Problematik der Jesusfrage." *Evangelische Theologie* 29 (1969): 453–476.

Thielicke, Helmut. "Autorität." In *Religion in Geschichte und Gegenwart*, vol. 1, ed. Kurt Galling. 3d ed. Tübingen: J. C. B. Mohr, 1957: 792–794.

Tillich, Paul. *Systematic Theology*, vol. 1. Chicago: University of Chicago Press, 1951.

_____. *Gesammelte Werke*, vol. 1: *Frühe Hauptwerke*. Stuttgart: Evangelisches Verlagswerk, 1959.

Tracy, David. *Blessed Rage for Order: The New Pluralism in Theology*. New York: Seabury Press, 1975.

_____. *The Analogical Imagination: Christian Theology and the Culture of Pluralism*. New York: Crossroad Publishing Co., 1981.

Wesley, John. *Standard Sermons*, ed. Edward H. Sugden. London: Epworth Press, 1921.

Whitehead, Alfred North. *Religion in the Making*. New York: Macmillan Co., 1926.

_____. *The Function of Reason*. Princeton, NJ: Princeton University Press, 1929.

_____. *Adventures of Ideas*. New York: Macmillan Co., 1933.

_____. *Modes of Thought*. New York: Macmillan Co., 1938.

_____. *Process and Reality: An Essay in Cosmology*, ed. David Ray Griffin and Donald W. Sherburne. New York: Free Press, 1978.

Wittgenstein, Ludwig. *Philosophical Investigations*. 2d ed. Oxford: Basil Blackwell & Mott, 1958.

Index